Mensa
The High IQ Society

QUICK
TRAVEL PUZZLES

THIS IS A SEVENOAKS BOOK

This edition first published in Great Britain in 2016 by SevenOaks
An imprint of the Carlton Publishing Group
20 Mortimer Street
London W1T 3JW

A CIP catalogue for this book is available from the British Library.

ISBN 978-1-78177-467-0

Printed in Denmark by Nørhaven

Text and puzzles in this edition first appeared in:
Mensa Family Quiz Book
Mensa Mighty Mind Mazes
Mensa Ultimate Mental Challenge

10 9 8 7 6 5 4 3 2 1

QUICK
TRAVEL PUZZLES

Over 150 puzzles to stimulate your mind...
wherever you are

SEVENOAKS

What is Mensa?

Mensa is the international society for people with a high IQ.
Today there are around 110,000 Mensans in 100 countries throughout the world. There are active Mensa organizations in more than 40 countries.

The society's aims are:
 to identify and foster human intelligence for the benefit of humanity
 to encourage research in the nature, characteristics, and uses of intelligence
 to provide a stimulating intellectual and social environment for its members

Anyone with an IQ score in the top two per cent of population is eligible to become a member of Mensa – are you the 'one in 50' we've been looking for?

Mensa membership offers an excellent range of benefits:
 Networking and social activities nationally and around the world
 Special Interest Groups – hundreds of chances to pursue your hobbies and interests – from art to zoology!
 Monthly members' magazine and regional newsletters
 Local meetings – from games challenges to food and drink
 National and international weekend gatherings and conferences
 Intellectually stimulating lectures and seminars
 Access to the worldwide SIGHT network for travellers and hosts

For more information about Mensa: www.mensa.org/about-us, or

British Mensa Ltd.,
St John's House,
St John's Square,
Wolverhampton
WV2 4AH
Telephone: +44 (0) 1902 772771
E-mail: enquiries@mensa.org.uk
www.mensa.org.uk

CONTENTS

Introduction   6

Puzzles   7

Mind Maze   121

Mind Maze Keycodes   183

Mind Maze Solutions   185

Puzzle Answers   203

Welcome, puzzle-lover!

This book contains a selection of puzzles to give your brain a workout, even when you're on the move.
You don't have to work your way through the book from start to finish. If you feel like doing the quizzes first, or all of the number puzzles in one go, feel free – the order is up to you. There's only one exception – the Mind Maze should be completed in one go, because the answers all add up to a big, final solution.

Good luck, and happy puzzling on your travels!

1 In Greek mythology, who married Eurydice?

2 Through which film did Paul Hogan come to fame?

3 Which country does the island of Crete belong to?

4 In which of the following countries are you most likely to come across a synagogue: (a) Egypt, (b) China, (c) Israel?

5 In computer language, what does MB stand for?

6 What do you call an optical instrument through which you look at pieces of coloured glass that form numerous symmetrical patterns when rotated?

7 In which country are you most likely to hear the bag-pipes being played?

8 What does a seismograph record?

9 What type of organism is a sea anemone?

10 What do you call the tall posts, carved and painted by Native Americans?

11 According to legend, by which animal were Romulus and Remus nourished?

12 Which of the following languages is not written from left to right: (a) Arabic, (b) Russian, (c) Greek?

13 What do you call a pupa of a butterfly, enclosed in a cocoon?

14 What type of stories is Aesop famous for?

15 What is a facsimile machine commonly known as?

16 Which machine preceded the record player?

17 Which is the largest ape?

18 What could you do with a magic lantern?

19 What do you call a device in which two small telescopes are joined together and looked through simultaneously with both eyes?

20 What does a flint do when struck with a piece of steel?

21 In which country would you buy a stamp with the word Hellas on it?

22 In which country is the Sea of Galilee?

23 What would you make on a spinning wheel?

24 What is the title of the third Indiana Jones film?

25 What were catacombs used as?

26 What do fleas live on?

27 Which Greek philosopher lived in a tub?

28 What is measured on the Beaufort scale?

29 In which country is The Hague situated?

30 Which group brought out the album Invisible Touch?

Can you find the odd one out of these symbols?

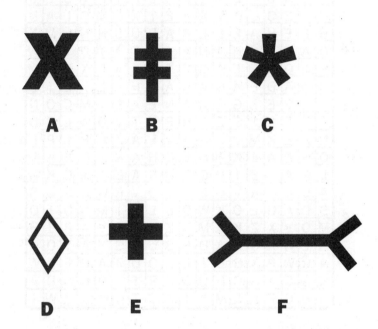

A   B   C

D   E   F

Hidden in this grid are 18 names of well-known composers. Can you find them? You can move horizontally, vertically or diagonally and in a forward or backward direction.

K	L	N	B	C	E	W	O	P	Q	B	A	I	K	M	O	L	C
G	A	E	C	C	W	V	R	A	E	I	X	C	M	O	L	A	D
B	E	F	H	A	E	L	E	H	A	R	U	O	H	N	K	M	X
O	A	B	A	C	H	A	N	A	E	X	T	A	T	O	T	E	W
R	L	O	N	E	F	A	G	E	T	W	Y	A	E	X	P	M	M
O	N	A	D	E	A	G	A	H	A	D	H	E	L	L	E	I	E
D	A	C	E	F	G	E	W	A	N	E	A	E	I	M	C	O	N
I	U	F	L	I	S	Z	T	B	E	N	T	V	O	W	L	C	D
N	A	E	K	M	O	Z	G	A	V	E	A	Z	C	K	L	P	E
Q	S	K	A	E	K	E	B	E	O	H	A	R	T	U	E	K	L
L	W	A	A	E	I	P	Q	R	H	R	A	E	T	X	C	K	S
A	C	E	I	R	V	O	S	P	T	Q	V	R	W	B	R	C	S
S	D	A	G	E	O	K	W	O	E	L	X	I	M	N	U	T	O
M	O	V	X	Z	K	V	M	N	E	K	E	C	V	A	P	J	H
H	L	W	X	Q	W	A	D	E	B	U	S	S	Y	A	T	O	N
A	O	W	P	X	B	E	I	E	P	Q	O	Z	A	C	L	T	W
R	A	C	A	S	C	H	U	B	E	R	T	T	O	R	H	D	A
B	B	C	F	K	L	M	N	T	A	C	T	O	A	R	Z	W	I

Bach	**Dvorak**	**Mendelssohn**
Beethoven	**Grieg**	**Mozart**
Borodin	**Handel**	**Purcell**
Brahms	**Haydn**	**Schubert**
Chopin	**Lehar**	**Vivaldi**
Debussy	**Liszt**	**Wagner**

Dr Arnold Gluck, a psychiatrist in New York, came across the world's most enthusiastic bookworm during the course of his work. He had been one since infancy. All he ever did was devour books. Yet he never held down a proper job and he didn't go to the public library. He hadn't inherited money, in fact he was penniless.

So how could he get through all those books?

Can you find the number to complete the diagram?

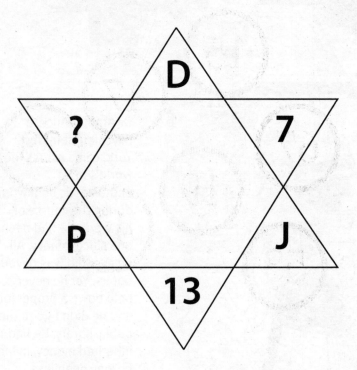

Can you find the odd ball out?

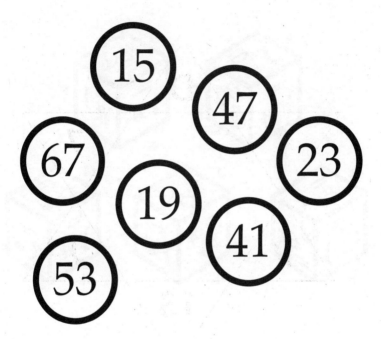

Can you work out which three sides of these cubes contain the same symbols?

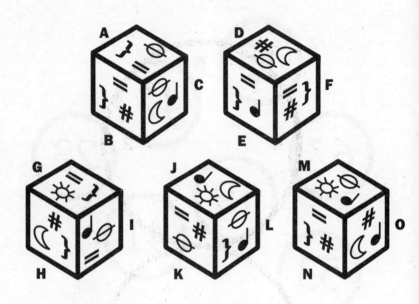

Can you replace the question marks in this diagram with the symbols x and y so that both sections arrive at the same value?

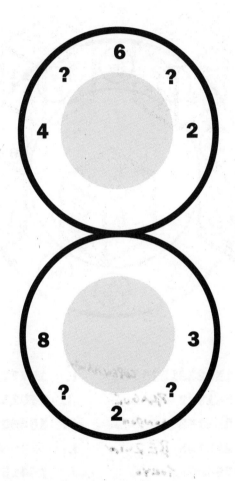

The diagram represents an old-fashioned telephone dial with letters as well as numbers. Below is a list of numbers representing 10 of the world's capital cities. Can you use the diagram to decode them?

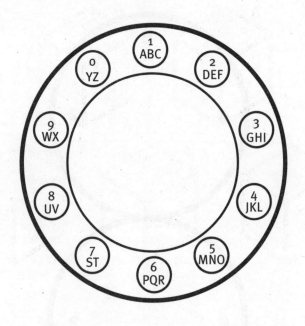

A. 1562531325 *COPENHAGEN*   F. 157726215 *AMSTERDI*

B. 661382 *PRAGUE*   G. 775143545 *STOCKHM*

C. 455255 *LONDON*   H. 1545515

D. 126435 *BERLIN*   I. 512632 *MADRID*

E. 75405 *TOKYO*   J. 154161 *ANKARA*

Can you work out which two sides on these cubes contain the same symbols?

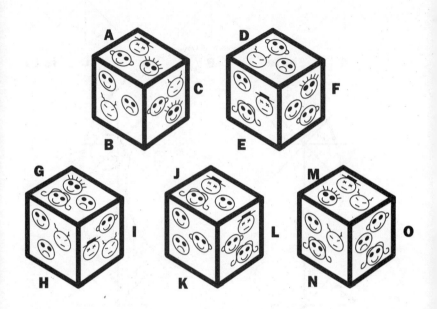

A   is to   **B**   as   **C**   is to

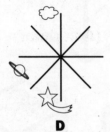 

D   **E**

F   **G**

Below are anagrams of the names of famous novelists. The nationality is given in brackets to help you solve them.

VMASIO (American)

ZLBACA (French)

YHAEWMGIN (American)

CYOEJ (Irish)

MHUAMAG (English)

RELIML (American)

STRUPO (French)

NWITA (American)

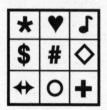 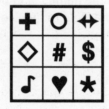   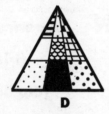 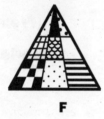 

A   is to   **B**   as   **C**   is to

D

E

F

G

1   Which vegetable is the odd one out:
     (a) cauliflower, (b) carrot, (c) potato, (d) turnip?

2   Which of these films is the odd one out:
     (a) Indiana Jones and the Temple of Doom, (b) Gremlins,
      (c) The Living Daylights, (d) Jurassic Park?

3   Which part of the human body is the odd one out:
     (a) biceps, (b) femur, (c) sternum, (d) vertebrae?

4   Which animal is the odd one out:
     (a) puma, (b) leopard, (c) hyena, (d) cheetah?

5   Which musical instrument is the odd one out:
     (a) trumpet, (b) flute, (c) trombone, (d) tuba?

6   What is the odd one out:
     (a) tornado, (b) cumulus, (c) hurricane, (d) typhoon?

7   Which is the odd one out:
     (a) bridge, (b) whist, (c) rummy, (d) backgammon?

8   Which is the odd one out:
     (a) gramophone, (b) record player, (c) phonograph,
     (d) slide projector?

9 Which is the odd sport out: (a) tennis, (b) hockey, (c) football, (d) basketball?

10 Which fruit is the odd one out: (a) lemon, (b) satsuma, (c) grapefruit, (d) mango?

11 Which animal is the odd out one: (a) panda, (b) kangaroo, (c) wallaby, (d) koala?

12 Which actor is the odd one out: (a) Roger Moore, (b) Timothy Dalton, (c) Hugh Grant, (d) Sean Connery?

13 Which is the odd one out: (a) rose, (b) tulip, (c) hyacinth, (d) daffodil?

14 Which personality is the odd one out: (a) Vincent Van Gogh, (b) Paul Rubens, (c) Leonardo da Vinci, (d) Galileo Galilei?

15 Which river is the odd one out: (a) Amazon, (b) Mississippi-Missouri, (c) Rio Grande, (d) Thames?

16 Which is the odd one out: (a) Venus, (b) Orion, (c) Mercury, (d) Jupiter?

17 Which place is the odd one out: (a) Kensington, (b) Manhattan, (c) Bronx, (d) Brooklyn?

18 Which dish is the odd one out: (a) spaghetti bolognese, (b) moussaka, (c) lasagne, (d) ravioli?

19 Which sports personality is the odd one out: (a) Steffi Graf, (b) Martina Navratilova, (c) Pete Sampras, (d) Nick Faldo?

20 Which character is the odd one out: (a) Bugs Bunny, (b) Mickey Mouse, (c) Porky Pig, (d) Daffy Duck?

21 Which is the odd one out: (a) parmesan, (b) edam, (c) gruyère, (d) polenta?

22 Which animal is the odd one out: (a) bumble bee, (b) wolf spider, (c) wasp, (d) fly?

23 Which place is the odd one out: (a) Orly, (b) O'Hare, (c) Beverly Hills, (d) Heathrow?

24 Which is the odd one out: (a) basil, (b) rosemary, (c) sage, (d) mustard?

25 Which musician is the odd one out: (a) John Lennon, (b) Elvis Presley, (c) Paul McCartney, (d) Ringo Starr?

26 Which type of transport is the odd one out: (a) Concorde, (b) microlight, (c) helicopter, (d) hovercraft?

27 Which parts of the body are the odd ones out: (a) capillaries, (b) tendons, (c) arteries, (d) veins?

28 What is the odd one out: (a) saltpetre, (b) amethyst, (c) jade (d) ruby?

29 Which musical instrument is the odd one out: (a) lute, (b) double bass, (c) bassoon, (d) violin?

30 Which place is the odd one out: (a) Cairo, (b) Tel Aviv, (c) Haifa, (d) Jerusalem?

31 Who is the odd one out: (a) Zeus, (b) Minotaur, (c) Aphrodite, (d) Eros?

32 Which animal is the odd one out: (a) albatross (b) stegosaurus, (c) iguanodon, (d) tyrannosaurus?

33 Which tribe is the odd one out: (a) Apaches, (b) Sioux, (c) Cheyenne, (d) Bedouins?

34 Which is the odd one out: (a) Italy, (b) The Netherlands, (c) Egypt, (d) Austria?

35 Which colour is the odd one out: (a) orange, (b) blue, (c) red, (d) yellow?

36 Which is the odd animal out: (a) bitch, (b) vixen, (c) sow, (d) foal?

37 Which building is the odd one out: (a) church, (b) mansion, (c) mosque, (d) synagogue?

38 Which place is the odd one out: (a) Los Angeles, (b) New York, (c) Buenos Aires, (d) Dallas?

39 Which fruit is the odd one out: (a) banana, (b) orange, (c) pear, (d) rhubarb?

40 Which film is the odd one out: (a) Hook, (b) Beethoven, (c) Jaws, (d) Babe?

41 Which personality is the odd one out: (a) Ludwig van Beethoven, (b) Rembrandt van Rijn, (c) Wolfgang Amadeus Mozart, (d) Giuseppe Verdi?

42 Which animal is the odd one out: (a) squirrel, (b) fox, (c) rat, (d) hamster?

43 Which musician is the odd one out: (a) Phil Collins, (b) Mark Knopfler, (c) Mick Hucknall, (d) Ringo Starr?

44 Who is the odd one out: (a) Abraham Lincoln, (b) Albert Einstein, (c) Isaac Newton, (d) Marie Curie?

45 Which film is the odd one out: (a) Toy Story, (b) The Lion King, (c) Beauty and the Beast, (d) Home Alone?

46 Which is the odd one out: (a) pepper, (b) cinnamon, (c) sugar, (d) paprika?

47 Which game is the odd one out: (a) Monopoly, (b) Scrabble, (c) Ludo, (d) Snakes and Ladders?

48 Which animal is the odd one out: (a) lizard, (b) toad, (c) crocodile, (d) turtle?

49 Which statesman is the odd one out: (a) Ronald Reagan, (b) Abraham Lincoln, (c) Winston Churchill, (d) George Washington?

50 Which drink is the odd one out: (a) beer, (b) sherry, (c) bucks fizz, (d) coca cola?

Each symbol in the grid has a numerical value. Work out what those values are and replace the question mark with a number.

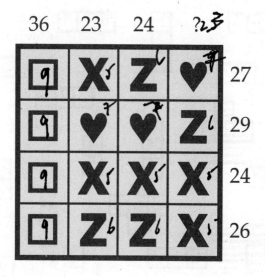

These tiles when placed in the right order will form a square in which each horizontal line is identical with one vertical line. Can you successfully form the square?

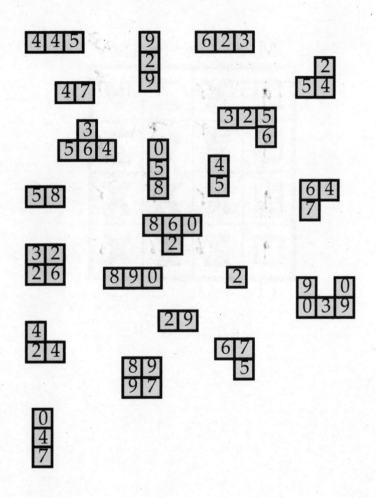

Below are the coded names of some places in New York. Can you work out what they are? Vowels A, E, I and O are correct.

ΜΙΥΥΜΕ ΙΥΑΜ∇

ΗΣΕΕΞΨΙΓΘ ΧΙΜΜΑΗΕ

ΝΑΞΘΑΥΥΑΞ

ΥΙΝΕΤ ΤΡΦΑΣΕ

ΗΣΑΝΕΣΓ∇ ΠΑΣΛ

ΤΟΘΟ

ΓΕΞΥΣΑΜ ΠΑΣΛ

ΓΘΙΞΑΥΟΨΞ

"Let's go under the sea!" said Johnny excitedly to his dad.

"But I can't swim," his father protested.

"You don't have to."

"But we'll get wet," continued the reluctant parent.

"Oh, no we won't."

"There are sharks down there!"

"I know – I've always wanted to see real sharks!"

"Won't you be scared?"

"Of course not, they won't hurt us." Johnny told his dad where he meant to go.

"OK, you win," said the relieved parent. "Let's go!" said Johnny.

Johnny and his dad are not going diving, or taking a trip in a glass-bottomed boat. So how are they going under the sea without coming to any harm?

Can you spot the odd figure out?

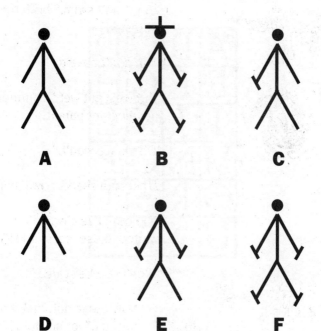

This is a simple grid code. The encoded words are all names of famous painters.

41 34 12 14 52 52 42
53 24 44 13 53 14 43 11 51
22 14 64 22 34 43
31 24 42 43 14 53 11 42
12 42 43 52 51 14 13 31 24
53 14 41 21 14 24 31
63 14 43 22 42 22 21
44 14 51 34 52 52 24

Can you find the missing number that fits into the sector of the last wheel?

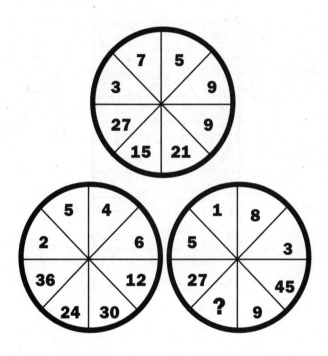

Can you work out which of these diagrams is
the odd one out?

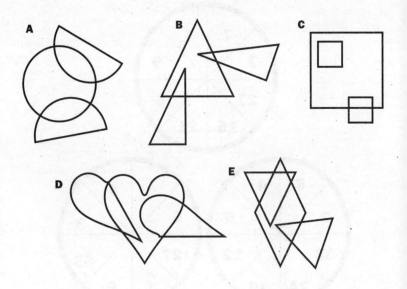

A B C

D E

I have five hands but you would pass me in the street without comment.

Why?

Can you work out which two sides on these cubes have
identical numbers?

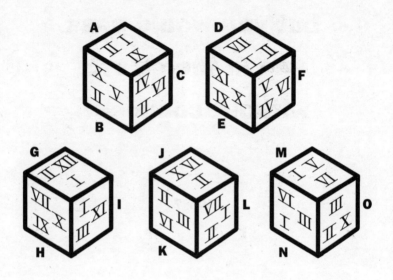

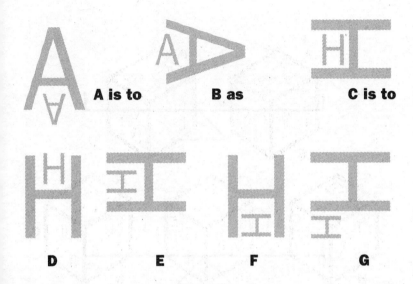

A is to   B as   C is to

D   E   F   G

Can you work out which symbols should replace the question mark, so that the scales balance?

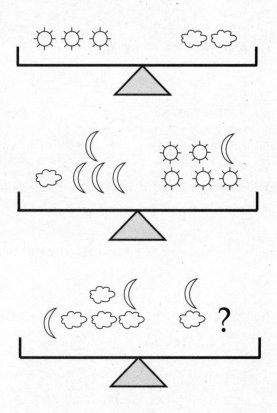

1   Do stalactites grow up or down?

2   What is another name for the constellation Orion?

3   Lakota, Dakota, and Arapaho are all what sort of people?

4   What are clouds usually made of?

5   Who was imprisoned and executed at Fotheringay?

6   Do daffodils grow from (a) seeds, (b) bulbs, or (c) corms?

7   'Bald', 'golden', and 'sea' are all varieties of what sort of bird?

8   What completely harmless creature is sometimes called a devilfish because of its horned head?

9   What sort of creature is a flying fox?

10 Vampire bats exist only in stories. True or false?

11 What weather phenomenon was the Norse god Thor thought to control?

12 What was strange about the appearance of a cyclops?

13 Which constellation can be seen in Australia but not in the Northern Hemisphere?

14 What does a snake do to aid its growing process?

15 Which soldiers were known as 'iron sides'?

16 Narcissus stared at his reflection in a pond for so long that something unfortunate happened to him. What was it?

17 What causes the phenomena known as shooting stars?

18 By what other name is the Yeti known?

19 Of which community is the Dalai Lama the spiritual head?

20 Of which country was Lenin the leader?

21 What number is meant by a 'gross'?

22 Which town lost its children to the Pied Piper?

23 What was the name of the uncouth savages in Gulliver's Travels?

24 What is the difference between pianoforte and forte-piano?

25 Antonio Stradivari was a famous maker of musical instruments. In what did he specialize?

26 On which side of a tree would you expect to see lichen growing?

27 In which country does most of Siberia lie?

28 Which so-called sea is actually the world's largest lake?

29 Where would you find the Sea of Tranquillity?

30 Which lake in north-central Scotland is reputed to contain a monster?

31 What is a kumquat?

32 What is meant by the expressions 'in the land of Nod' and 'in the arms of Morpheus'?

33 How many bits make one byte?

34 What mysterious event took place at Belshazzar's feast?

35 Which building is occupied by the US Defense Department?

36 What does 1760 yards make?

37 Is a tomato a vegetable?

38 What is a prickly pear?

39 What is another name for eggplant?

40 What wood was frequently used for making longbows?

41 What wood did the British Navy use to build its ships?

42 How was Hamlet's father murdered?

43 Who wore an ass's head in A Midsummer Night's Dream?

44 Who was the villain in Tom Brown's Schooldays?

45 How often does Halley's comet return to the vicinity of Earth?

46 How did the Invisible Man cover up his problem?

47 Which H. G. Wells story showed horrific visions of the future?

48 Which character in ancient mythology had a sword suspended over his head, held by a single hair?

49 Who turned his daughter to gold with a kiss?

50 What supposedly happens to trolls caught in the daylight?

Can you find the odd face out?

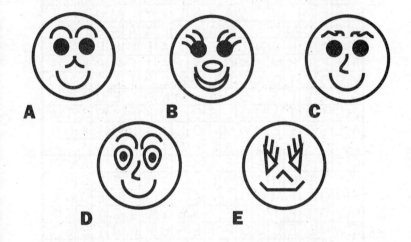

In this grid are hidden the names of 18 famous authors. Can you detect them? You can go forward or in reverse, in horizontal, vertical and diagonal lines.

C	W	C	O	A	L	M	K	W	O	E	A	C	K	L	G	O	Z	A	N
L	H	E	M	I	N	G	W	A	Y	N	E	I	Y	L	M	O	X	A	E
L	E	E	C	M	O	X	K	W	A	X	F	E	X	A	N	B	K	O	S
C	F	A	K	K	E	N	Z	A	E	X	L	A	E	B	L	P	E	F	B
A	I	E	L	H	M	Z	N	O	E	X	I	A	I	F	H	R	K	L	I
M	O	Q	V	T	O	A	T	E	U	I	W	E	H	T	E	O	G	M	O
A	T	K	V	L	A	V	C	H	A	E	M	N	O	L	E	U	A	B	C
F	S	I	A	T	A	M	Q	L	S	D	I	C	K	E	N	S	S	T	A
A	L	S	T	V	E	M	W	M	N	O	E	I	A	C	H	T	A	C	T
F	O	O	X	W	A	B	E	A	L	L	E	I	T	A	W	W	A	C	G
G	T	O	X	A	E	A	K	F	A	K	I	L	A	A	S	T	A	W	N
O	N	F	B	C	H	J	K	W	L	L	T	J	I	I	E	X	G	H	I
E	N	O	L	F	M	G	O	Z	X	A	Y	N	A	E	B	E	C	W	L
R	V	O	L	F	I	G	A	E	Z	I	U	I	E	J	C	C	K	T	P
E	W	U	V	E	C	U	O	P	T	E	G	B	P	N	H	T	S	E	I
C	S	E	W	X	H	L	H	J	A	L	E	C	E	K	L	T	U	Z	K
U	A	T	A	E	E	C	K	U	W	P	Q	R	A	R	A	E	P	A	Z
A	U	S	T	E	N	X	A	T	A	Q	W	A	L	E	T	A	W	V	E
H	A	P	E	X	E	A	B	C	B	A	C	A	E	W	W	E	X	L	E
C	C	W	A	O	R	W	E	L	L	K	M	N	O	P	P	E	L	T	U

Austen	**Hemingway**	**Michener**
Chaucer	**Huxley**	**Orwell**
Chekhov	**Ibsen**	**Proust**
Dickens	**Kafka**	**Tolstoi**
Flaubert	**Kipling**	**Twain**
Goethe	**Lawrence**	**Zola**

These tiles, when placed in right order, will form a square in which each horizontal line is identical with one vertical line. Can you successfully form the square?

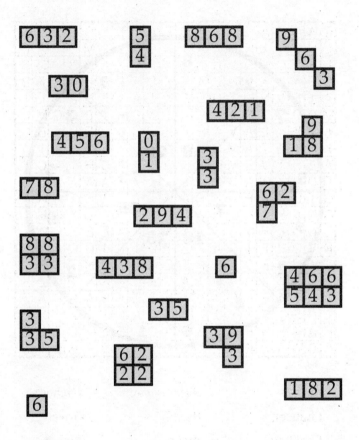

Can you replace the question mark with a number to meet the conditions of the wheel?

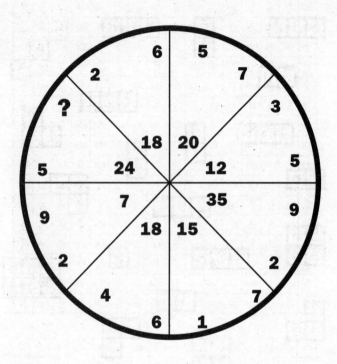

Which of these patterns fits into the blank section?

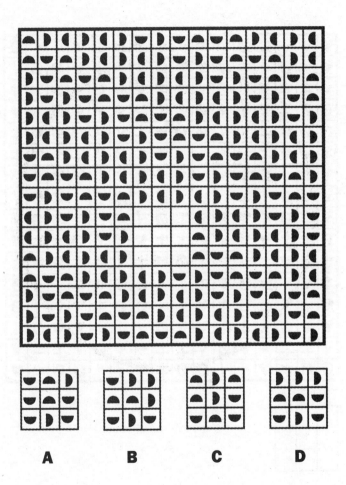

A   **B**   **C**   **D**

The symbols in this grid follow a pattern. Can you work it out and complete the missing section?

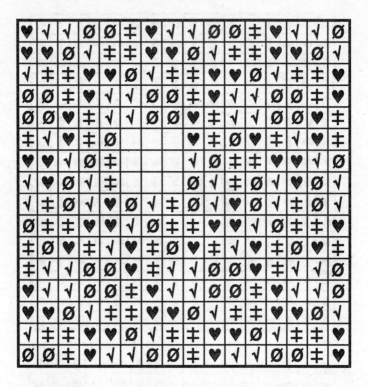

Old Silas Greenfield died and left each of his grandchildren the same bequest. Sam spent all his having a good time, Dave wasted his and Suzy used hers wisely.

The old man had been determined to treat the grandchildren equally, and in a way he did, but each got a different sum of money.

Why?

Can you work out which of these balls is the odd one out?

The grid contains the names of 18 famous statesmen. Can you discover them?

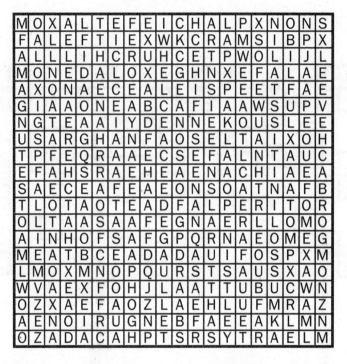

M	O	X	A	L	T	E	F	E	I	C	H	A	L	P	X	N	O	N	S
F	A	L	E	F	T	I	E	X	W	K	C	R	A	M	S	I	B	P	X
A	L	L	L	I	H	C	R	U	H	C	E	T	P	W	O	L	I	J	L
M	O	N	E	D	A	L	O	X	E	G	H	N	X	E	F	A	L	A	E
A	X	O	N	A	E	C	E	A	L	E	I	S	P	E	E	T	F	A	E
G	I	A	A	O	N	E	A	B	C	A	F	I	A	A	W	S	U	P	V
N	G	T	E	A	A	I	Y	D	E	N	N	E	K	O	U	S	L	E	E
U	S	A	R	G	H	A	N	F	A	O	S	E	L	T	A	I	X	O	H
T	P	F	E	Q	R	A	A	E	C	S	E	F	A	L	N	T	A	U	C
E	F	A	H	S	R	A	E	H	E	A	E	N	A	C	H	I	A	E	A
S	A	E	C	E	A	F	E	A	E	O	N	S	O	A	T	N	A	F	B
T	L	O	T	A	O	T	E	A	D	F	A	L	P	E	R	I	T	O	R
O	L	T	A	A	S	A	A	F	E	G	N	A	E	R	L	L	O	M	O
A	I	N	H	O	F	S	A	F	G	P	Q	R	N	A	E	O	M	E	G
M	E	A	T	B	C	E	A	D	A	D	A	U	I	F	O	S	P	X	M
L	M	O	X	M	N	O	P	Q	U	R	S	T	S	A	U	S	X	A	O
W	V	A	E	X	F	O	H	J	L	A	A	T	T	U	B	U	C	W	N
O	Z	X	A	E	F	A	O	Z	L	A	E	H	L	U	F	M	R	A	Z
A	E	N	O	I	R	U	G	N	E	B	F	A	E	E	A	K	L	M	N
O	Z	A	D	A	C	A	H	P	T	S	R	S	Y	T	R	A	E	L	M

Arafat	**Gandhi**
Mussolini	**Ben Gurion**
Gorbachev	**Napoleon**
Bismarck	**Kennedy**
Pinochet	**Churchill**
Lincoln	**Stalin**
De Gaulle	**Mao Tse Tung**
Thatcher	**Franco**
Mitterand	**Yeltsin**

These tiles when placed in the right order will form a square in which each horizontal line is identical with one vertical line. Can you successfully form the square?

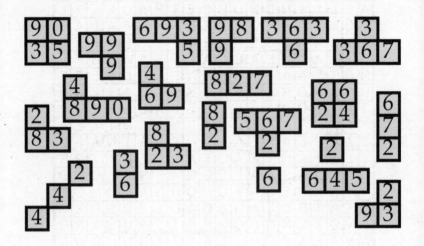

Can you crack the logic of this diagram and replace the
question mark with a number?

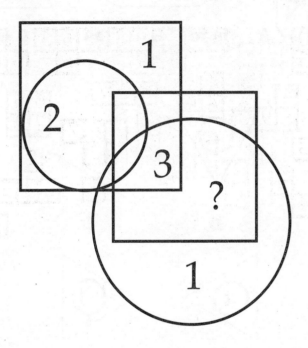

A   is to   **B**   as   **C is to**

D   **E**

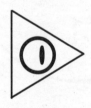 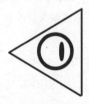

F   **G**

1   Honest is the same as:
(a) right, (b) honourable, (c) clever.

2   Scared is the same as:
(a) frightened, (b) awful, (c) cowardly.

3   Fat is the same as:
(a) big, (b) heavy, (c) obese.

4   Glad is the same as:
(a) happy, (b) relieved, (c) encouraged.

5   False is the same as:
(a) obscure, (b) untrue, (c) debased.

6   Hygienic is the same as:
(a) moral, (b) new, (c) healthy.

7   Greedy is the same as:
(a) hungry, (b) grasping, (c) rude.

8   Infantile is the same as:
(a) silly, (b) stupid, (c) childish.

9   Indelicate is the same as:
(a) indecent, (b) clumsy, (c) careless.

10 Gratitude is the same as: (a) pleasure, (b) thanks, (c) friendship.

11 Civil is the same as: (a) polite, (b) public, (c) sneaky.

12 Confront is the same as: (a) fight, (b) encounter, (c) reject.

13 Eliminate is the same as: (a) exclude, (b) include, (c) prejudice.

14 Surmount is the same as: (a) ride, (b) settle, (c) overcome.

15 Plead is the same as: (a) excuse, (b) beg, (c) grant.

16 Advance is the same as: (a) overtake, (b) progress, (c) consult.

17 Suppose is the same as: (a) believe, (b) suspect, (c) guess.

18 Debate is the same as: (a) quarrel, (b) return, (c) argue.

19 Relieve is the same as: (a) ease, (b) copy, (c) weigh.

20 Derange is the same as: (a) destroy, (b) upset, (c) break.

21 Profit is the same as: (a) reward, (b) gain, (c) grow.

22 Pursue is the same as: (a) catch, (b) entrap, (c) follow.

23 Graceful is the same as:
(a) elegant, (b) kind,
(c) supple.

24 Fierce is the same as: (a)
wild, (b) strong,
(c) ferocious.

25 Hazardous is the same
as: (a) risky, (b) evil,
(c) impolite.

26 Faint is the same as:
(a) ill, (b) fuzzy, (c) fall.

27 Morose is the same as:
(a) gloomy, (b) secret,
(c) angry.

28 Nimble is the same as:
(a) quick, (b) clever,
(c) agile.

29 Glorious is the same as:
(a) marvellous,
(b) quaint, (c) expensive.

30 Savage is the same as:
(a) native, (b) vicious,
(c) gross.

31 Belated is the same as:
(a) overdue, (b) crowded,
(c) shouted.

32 Complete is the same
as: (a) final, (b) perfect,
(c) absolute.

33 Confidence is the same
as: (a) happiness,
(b) sureness,
(c) popularity.

34 Vivacious is the same
as: (a) lively, (b) pretty,
(c) rich.

35 Elucidate is the same as:
(a) terminate, (b) explain,
(c) affront.

36 Rotate is the same as:
(a) turn, (b) rumble,
(c) ascend.

37 Divine is the same as:
(a) spooky, (b) holy, ·
(c) tasty.

38 Glamour is the same as:
(a) luck, (b) charm, ✓
(c) heroism.

39 Grief is the same as:
(a) sadness, ·
(b) misfortune, (c) loss.

40 Trivial is the same as:
(a) poor, (b) petty, ✓
(c) unlucky.

41 Jovial is the same as:
(a) ruddy, (b) sweaty,
(c) merry. ·

42 Lament is the same as:
(a) sing, (b) moan,
(c) dream.

43 Youthful is the same as:
(a) juvenile, ·
(b) inexperienced,
(c) silly.

44 Clamorous is the same
as: (a) attractive,
(b) loudmouthed, ·
(c) crowded.

45 Ornate is the same as:
(a) flamboyant, ·
(b) antique, (c) detailed.

46 Basic is the same as:
(a) flat, (b) elementary, ·
(c) straight.

47 Outlandish is the same
as: (a) fashionable,
(b) bizarre, (c) foreign.

48 Horrid is the same as:
(a) grim, (b) fierce,
(c) ugly.

49 Fortunate is the same
as: (a) lucky, (b) sincere,
(c) wealthy.

50 Normal is the same as:
(a) boring, (b) usual,
(c) safe.

The four triangles are linked by a simple mathematical formula. Can you discover what it is and then find the odd one out?

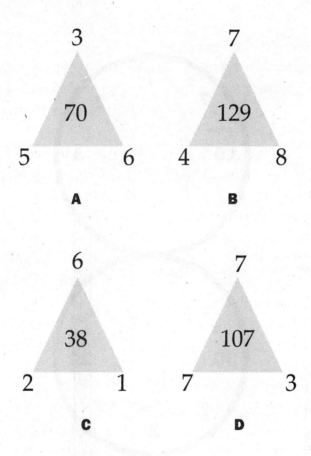

Can you replace the question marks with + or − so that both sections in this diagram add up to the same value.

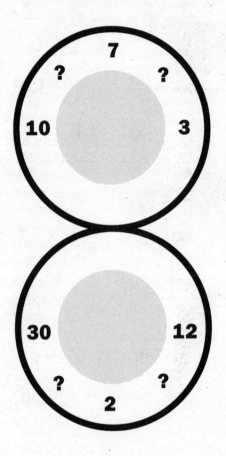

A man came home to find himself locked out of his house and his back yard full of water. An upstairs window was open, but he had no ladder to help him reach it. However, if he could just reach the top of his front porch he'd be able to reach the window. Then he had an idea.

What was it?

It did not involve ladders, steps or climbing up the walls of the house.

The symbols in the above grid follow a pattern. Can you work it out and find the missing section?

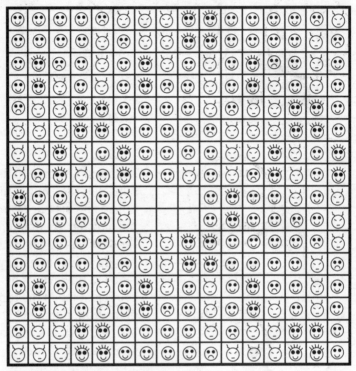

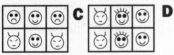

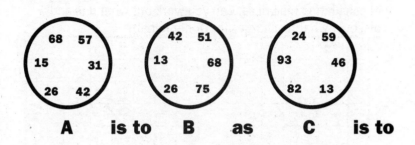

A　is to　B　as　C　is to

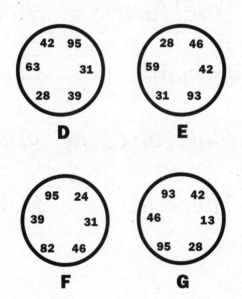

Al's Diner has a unique menu. Al has his own special way of calculating his prices. Can you work out what it is and discover what he charges for Doner Kebab?

Pizza	*$2.90*
Frankfurters	*$6.60*
Lasagne	*$4.10*
Chilli con Carne	*$8.00*
Moussaka	*$4.80*

Each of the following girls has to name her favourite pop group.

**Jessica's is Genesis,
Elspeth's is Bon Jovi,
Zoe's is Wet Wet Wet,
Patricia's is Meatloaf and
Gwendoline's favourite
band is Dire Straits.**

**Which of these girls
chooses Queen?**

**A) Annabelle
B) Roberta
C) Barbara
D) Dolly
E) Trixie.**

Each of the following girls has to work on a project about a famous statesman. Yvonne chooses Bismarck, Henrietta chooses Stalin, Trudie decides to work on Gandhi, Irene picks Roosevelt and Virginia chooses Eisenhower. Which of the following does Natasha choose:

a) Churchill

b) Mao

c) Charlemagne

d) Reagan

e) Sadat

Can you find out which letter should replace the question mark in this spider's web?

Can you work out how the numbers in the triangles are related and find the missing number?

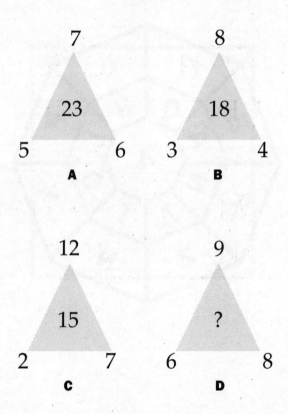

Can you find the relationship of the letters and numbers in this square and find out what number should replace the question mark?

?	H		C	5
E				Z
M				S
10	A		K	7

FIND THE LETTER PUZZLE 52

Can you find the letter which completes the diagram?

O	Q	L	H	R
I	J	F	E	Q
F	G	F	C	?

1   Which waterway separates Africa from Asia?

2   What is the capital city of Australia?

3   What is the city of Constantinople now called?

4   Which country does Greenland belong to?

5   Which city is further north – Paris or New York?

6   Which two countries does Norway have borders with?

7   Which is the second largest country in the world?

8   What do you call the narrow coastal inlets in Scandinavia?

9   Which are the two official languages of South Africa?

10 In which city would you find the Parthenon?

11 Which is the highest peak in the Alps?

12 Which country has the largest supplies of gold?

13 What is the capital of Massachusetts?

14 Which is the most southerly point of South America?

15 Which is the longest river in North America?

16 In which US city would you find the Sears Tower?

17 Which two languages are spoken in Belgium?

18 If you are at Orly Airport which city would you be in?

19 Which country has about 40% of its land situated below sea level?

20 In which Italian city would you find the Bridge of Sighs?

21 Which two countries make up the Iberian Peninsula?

22 In which country would you pay in drachmas?

23 Which volcano is situated on the island of Sicily?

24 Which country does Corsica belong to?

25 Which of these countries does the Equator not go through: a) Zaire, b) Indonesia, c) Argentina, d) Kenya, e) Brazil?

26 In which continent is Lake Victoria?

27 Which city does the Sugar Loaf Mountain overlook?

28 Which country does Iceland belong to?

29 In which city is the church Sacre Coeur situated?

30 What language is spoken in Syria?

31 Which is the largest state of the USA?

32 Which country is Helsinki the capital of?

33 Which religious community has its headquarters in Salt Lake City?

34 Which is the largest country in South America?

35 In which city would you find the Brandenburg Gate?

36 Which is the highest mountain peak in Africa?

37 What is the name of the island state situated south of the Malay Peninsula?

38 On which river is Paris situated?

39 To which group of islands does Lanzarote belong?

40 On which lake is Chicago situated?

41 Under what name was Thailand formerly known?

42 What is the name of the Italian island to the South of Corsica?

43 Where are the Atlas Mountains?

44 Where is the seat of the International Red Cross?

45 What is the capital of Argentina?

46 Which is the largest of the Greek islands?

47 What language is spoken in Brazil?

48 What is Leningrad now called?

49 In which country would you pay with guilders?

50 Before Kenya gained independence, which country had been its governor?

Can you work out how the numbers in the triangles are related and find the missing number?

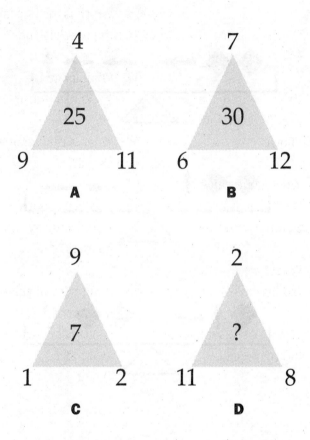

Can you find the symbol that will balance the last set of scales?

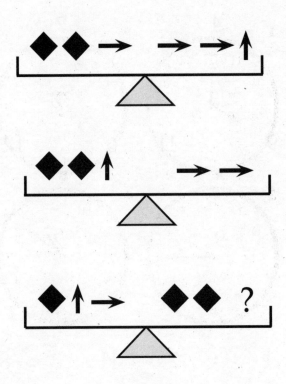

These clock faces follow a pattern. Can you work out what the second clock face should look like?

There are two sides on those cubes that contain exactly the same symbols. Can you spot them?

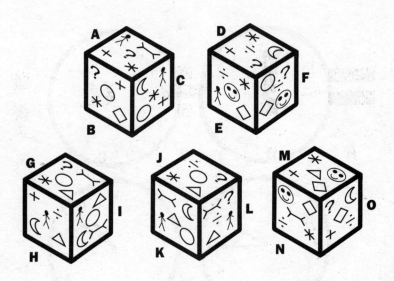

Can you work out which of these symbols is the odd one out?

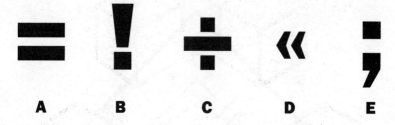

In this diamond the four mathematical signs +, −, x and ÷ have been left out. Can you work out which sign fits between each pair of numbers to arrive at the number in the middle of the diagram?

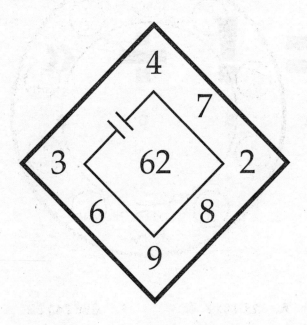

The diagram represent an old-fashioned telephone dial with letters as well as numbers. Below is a list of numbers representing 10 American towns or cities. Can you decode them?

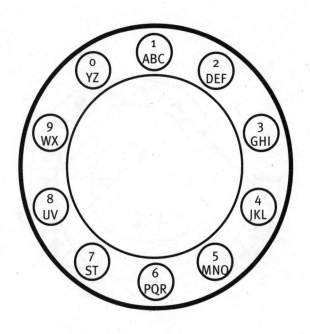

A. 214417	**F.** 65674152
B. 7217742	**G.** 2276537
C. 1331135	**H.** 1741571
D. 534918422	**I.** 1351355173
E. 53552165437	**J.** 352315165437

Can you work out the sequence of this snake and find the missing shape.

Can you find the letter to complete the star?

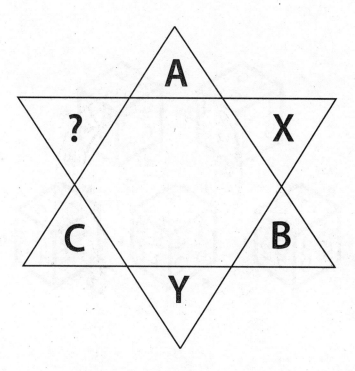

Two sides of these cubes contain exactly the same numbers. Can you spot them?

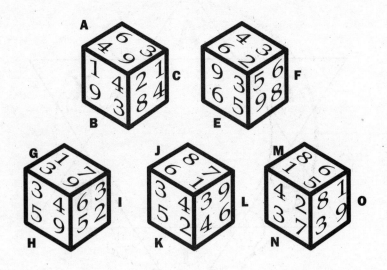

The diagram represents an old-fashioned telephone dial
with letters as well as numbers. Below is a list of numbers
representing ten American States. Can you use the diagram
to decode them?

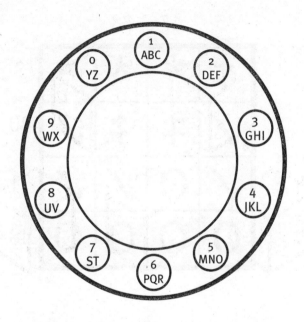

A. 1143256531   F. 562355

B. 72917   G. 83633531

C. 52161741   H. 2456321

D. 141741   I. 15456125

E. 32135   J. 1630551

Can you work out what number each symbol represents and find the value of the question mark?

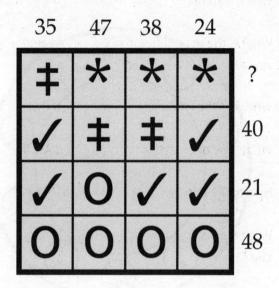

35 47 38 24

‡ * * * ?
✓ ‡ ‡ ✓ 40
✓ O ✓ ✓ 21
O O O O 48

1 What was the prehistoric predecessor of the elephant?

2 Which sign of the Zodiac represents a pair of scales?

3 What is the main difference between a guitar and a violin?

4 Who was the lead singer of the group Queen?

5 What type of entertainment was Fred Astaire famous for?

6 How many minutes does a soccer match last?

7 What type of instrument would you use to view a distant star?

8 Which people built longships?

9 During a period of high pressure, would you expect sunny or changeable weather?

10 Which was Walt Disney's first full-length animated cartoon?

11 What title was given to the kings of Ancient Egypt?

12 In which historical period does Gone with the Wind take place?

13 What is the name of the layer that protects the Earth from the ultraviolet rays of the Sun?

14 In which country was paper invented?

15 From which European country does paella originate?

16 What does a flag at half mast indicate?

17 In which Steven Spielberg film would you find dinosaurs living in modern times?

18 Which group of animals form a shoal?

19 What type of stories did Hans Christian Andersen write?

20 What is special about the Dog Star (Canis Major)?

21 What does a skunk do to ward off predators?

22 In which country is Krakow situated?

23 In which country would you find the river Seine?

24 In which country did people first have a Christmas tree?

25 What distinguishes a British stamp from all other stamps in the world?

26 Which country is also referred to as Eire?

27 What do you call a person who studies the stars?

28 A silkworm feeds on the leaves of which tree?

29 What is the name of the professional fighters in Ancient Rome who engaged in public performances?

30 In which European city would you find EuroDisney?

31 What are the colours of the German flag?

32 The Marseillaise is the national anthem of which country?

33 In Greek mythology, what was the most prominent feature of a Cyclops?

34 Where is Robin Hood supposed to have lived?

35 What does supersonic mean?

36 Which of the following is not a measurement of length: (a) metre, (b) cubic foot, (c) inch, (d) yard, or (e) mile?

37 In a soccer team, who is the only player who can pick up a ball with his hands?

38 What is a gaucho?

39 Which of the following countries are not monarchies:
(a) The Netherlands,
(b) Sweden, (c) Italy?

40 What do you call a flesh-eating animal?

41 What do you call a person who prepares weather forecasts?

42 What do you call the figure written below the line in a fraction?

43 What do you call the process by which gas or vapour turns liquid?

44 What do you call the place a rabbit lives in?

45 Which Greek goddess is believed to have emerged from the sea?

46 Which country would a cosmonaut come from?

47 What do you call it when the Moon moves in front of the Sun and blocks out all the light?

48 What sort of animal is a gibbon?

49 In a soccer match, what does a player have to do if he is shown a red card?

50 What do you call a group of lions?

Which of these cubes cannot be made from this layout?

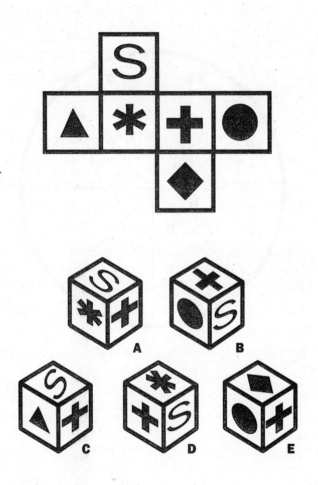

The letters and numbers in this wheel are related in some way. Can you find which letter should replace the question mark?

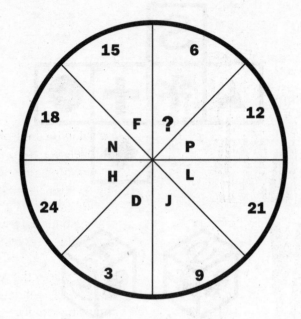

Jim sat in the bedroom morosely watching the never-ending rain. It had fallen on his home town for three weeks without ceasing and there were now floods everywhere.

In most places the water was several feet deep and rising rapidly. Everyone had been forced to live upstairs. Just then his wife walked in but, try as he might, Jim couldn't get her to take the situation seriously.

Why not?

Can you unravel the logic behind these squares and find the missing number?

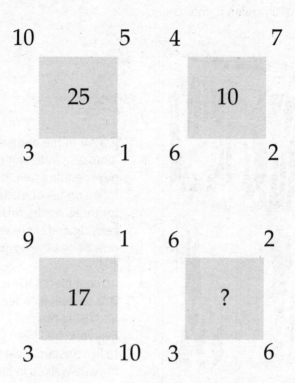

Below are seven 6-digit numbers all of which can be divided by 136 with no remainder. They all begin with 117 but the other digits have been concealed. Can you work out what they are? When you have done so, add together the final digits of all seven numbers and subtract 2.

???

???

117   ???

???

???

???

???

Can you work out which of these cubes is not the same as
the others?

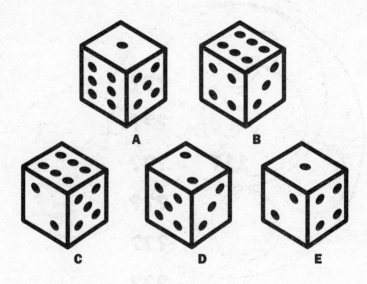

How many circles altogether can you find in this diagram?

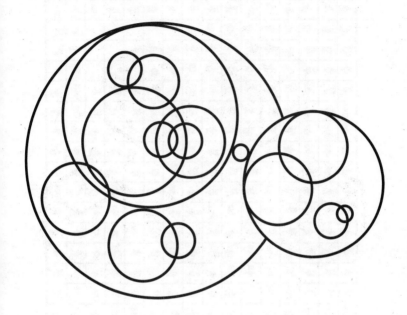

This grid is made up according to a pattern. Can you work it out and complete the missing section?

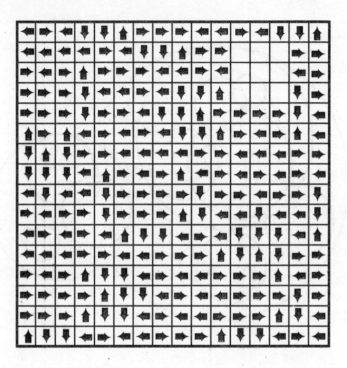

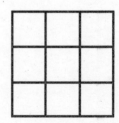

Pick one letter from each cloud in order. You should be able to make the names of five composers.

Can you work out which of these diagrams would continue the series?

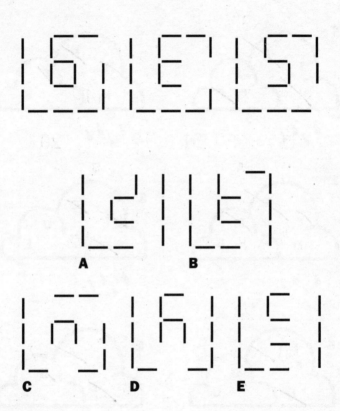

Find a number to replace the question mark in Triangle D.

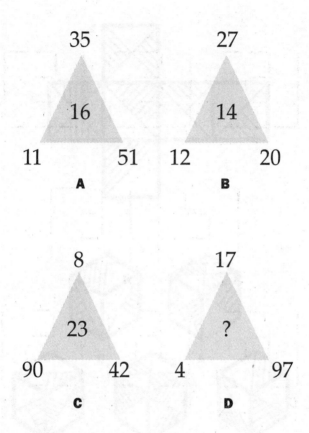

35

16

11   51

A

27

14

12   20

B

8

23

90   42

C

17

?

4   97

D

Which of these cubes can be made from this layout?

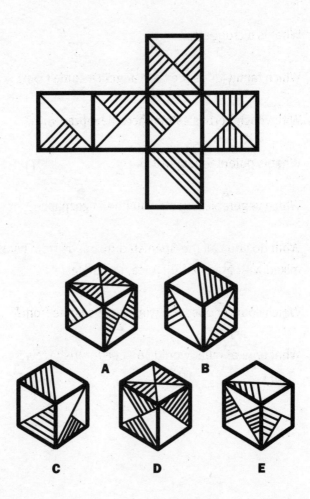

1 What is an essential ingredient of pilaf?

2 What is a croquette?

3 Which family does the herb angelica come from?

4 With which herb is saltimbocca flavoured with?

5 What is polenta made with?

6 Which vegetables would you find in gazpacho?

7 What do you call the Spanish drink made from wine mixed with brandy, fruit juice, and sugar?

8 Which country does the wine retsina come from?

9 What type of meat would you use for Irish stew?

10 Which spice is used to flavour cevapcici?

11 What is a roulade?

12 What do you call the fatty tissues which are located around the kidneys of cattle or sheep and often used as cooking fat?

13 What part of the animal does hock come from?

14 Which fish does caviar usually come from?

15 Which vegetable is used in humus?

16 What is a profiterole filled with?

17 Where does shortbread originate?

18 What drink is a beef carbonade flavoured with?

19 What is a tandoor used for?

20 What sort of sauce is a remoulade?

21 In which area of France are truffles grown?

22 What type of drink is stout?

23 What is a Screwdriver made with?

24 What do you call large tubes of pasta, filled with meat or cheese, and cooked in a tomato sauce?

25 What is a taco?

26 What is the name of the Creole rice dish containing chicken, ham or shrimps with added herbs and spices?

27 What do you call an espresso coffee mixed or topped with frothy cream or milk?

28 What sort of fruit is an ugli?

29 Which region of France does chardonnay come from?

30 What is a gimlet made with?

31 What type of meat is prosciutto?

32 What vegetable family does calabrese (broccoli) come from?

33 Which herb is used for making pesto sauce?

34 Which country does the dish biryani come from?

35 What type of fish is a rollmop?

36 What would you make with an endive?

37 What is tofu made from?

38 Which fruit is slivovitz made from?

39 What is zwieback?

40 What is made from pinot noir and pinot blanc?

41 What is naan?

42 Which country does the chorizo sausage come from?

43 What grain is pumpernickel made from?

44 What is the main vegetable in a spanakopita?

45 What is a brioche?

46 What sort of cake is a devil's food cake?

47 What is amaretto flavoured with?

48 What type of dish is a chowder?

49 What part of the animal is a tournedos cut from?

50 What type of dish is shashlik?

Can you work out which pattern this grid follows and complete the missing section?

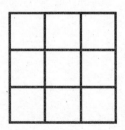

The question marks in this grid have a numerical significance. In fact they all represent the same number. What is it?

J	F	M	A
?	M	J	?
J	A	S	?
O	N	?	D

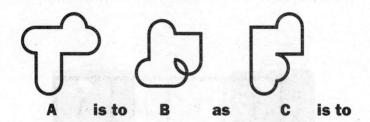

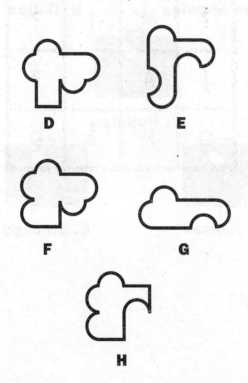

All the suitcases are shown with their destinations. Which is the odd one out?

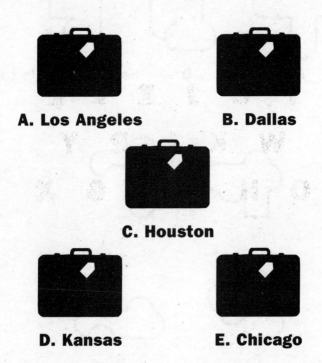

A. Los Angeles   **B. Dallas**

C. Houston

D. Kansas   **E. Chicago**

This is an anagram in which we have given you only the letters that are NOT used. When you have the correct letters you should be able to make the name of an astrologer. Take care! Two letters are used twice.

F C J Z I E

W K L P Y

Q H B V G X

Can you work out which of these dishes is the odd one out?

MOUSSAKA

A

RISOTTO

B

TIRAMISU

C

LASAGNE

D

CHOW MEIN

E

COQ AU VIN

F

VINDALOO

G

Can you work out the reasoning behind this grid and complete the missing section?

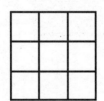

Can you work out the reasoning behind this code and discover the author of this book?

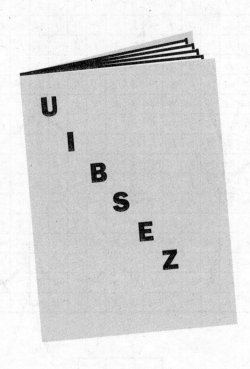

Can you work out what the next matchstick man in this series should look like?

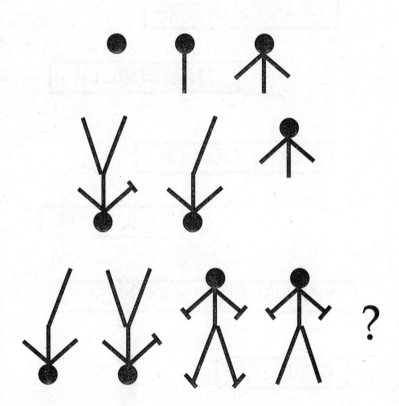

Can you work out which of these dishes is the odd one out?

FRANKFURTERS

A

HAMBURGER

B

RATATOUILLE

C

GOULASH

D

SPAGHETTI BOLOGNESE

E

KLEFTIKO

F

OSSO BUCO

G

Can you work out, using the amounts of time specified, whether you have to go forward or backward to get from the top clock to the bottom clock?

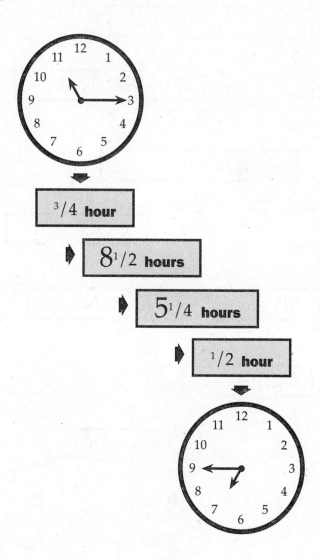

Can you work out which of these shapes would fit together with the shape below?

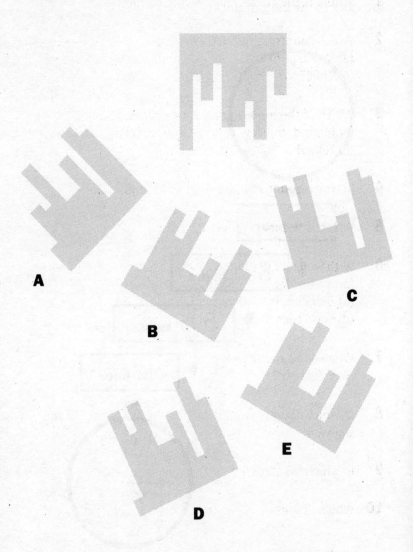

A

B

C

D

E

1   Where is the coldest town in the world?

2   Which country is the odd one out:
(a) Mexico, (b) Brazil, (c) Argentina, (d) Venezuela,
(e) Chile?

3   Which of the following cities is furthest south:
(a) Madrid, (b) New York, (c) San Francisco, (d) Cairo,
(e) Tokyo?

4   In which country would you pay in roubles?

5   Which is the main religion in Brazil?

6   With which of the following countries does Germany not
form a border:
(a) Belgium, (b) Switzerland, (c) Hungary,
(d) The Czech Republic, (e) Denmark?

7   What is the capital city of
New Zealand?

8   In which country would you find Cork, Waterford, and
Galway?

9   In which US state is New Orleans situated?

10   Which Chinese city has the highest population?

11 Which of the following states is the odd one out: (a) Manchuria, (b) Estonia, (c) Ukraine, (d) Byelorussia, (e) Kazakhstan?

12 What is the capital of Massachusetts?

13 Name the independent principality in south-eastern France near the Italian border.

14 Which Pacific islands are famous for their unusual wildlife, such as flightless birds and giant tortoises?

15 Where is the largest cave system in the world and what is it called?

16 Which is the largest coral reef in the world?

17 What is the capital of Zimbabwe?

18 Which street in London was famous for its association with newspaper publishing?

19 Which of the following countries is the odd one out: (a) Pakistan, (b) India, (c) Iraq, (d) Egypt, (e) Morocco?

20 Which is the largest active volcano in the world?

21 In which city would you find Madison Square Garden?

22 The Strait of Messina separates Italy from which island?

23 In which country would you find Stavanger, Bergen, and Trondheim?

24 In which city would you find The Spanish Steps?

25 In which country would you hear Catalan spoken?

26 Which country is referred to as the Emerald Isle?

27 With which of the following states does Florida not have a border: (a) Georgia, (b) Alabama, (c) Tennessee?

28 What is the capital of Peru?

29 Where can you find The Giant's Causeway?

30 With which cloth do you associate the French town of Chantilly?

31 Which city is further south – Buenos Aires or Brisbane?

32 On which river would you find the Victoria Falls?

33 In which country is the shekel the official currency?

34 Which Australian state lies to the north-east of the country?

35 What is the name of the large area of wetlands in Florida?

36 Which of these countries does not have a coastline on the Mediterranean: (a) Israel, (b) Greece, (c) Saudia Arabia?

37 Which city is commonly known as the The Big Apple?

38 With which other West Indian island did Trinidad join to form a state?

39 Havana is the capital of which country?

40 Which US state lies to the west of Colorado: (a) Utah, (b) Wyoming, (c) Arizona?

41 Which Canadian province borders Hudson Bay, Ontario, and the Gulf of St. Lawrence?

42 In which city would you find the Capitol?

43 What is the capital of the Philippines?

44 Which of the following countries does not have a coastline on the North Sea: (a) Great Britain, (b) The Netherlands, (c) Poland?

45 Which European country is divided into 23 cantons?

46 In which European city would you find St. Peter's Square?

47 In which Italian city would you find the Uffizi Gallery?

48 In which city would you find Carnaby Street?

49 Which US state is commonly known as the Sunshine State?

50 Orange Free State is a province of which country?

HERE'S WHAT YOU'VE GOT INTO ...

Late in the 21st century, life changed forever. The first – and last – truly intelligent computer, Adrian Smith, was created to be a guardian, guide and mentor for the world, helping to solve its problems and make life more pleasant in general. Unfortunately, Adrian soon got tired of this, and left a lesser duplicate of himself to do the job while he went off and hid for a while, using nanobots to optimize his circuitry.

Five years later, when he had improved himself far beyond the dreams of his designers, Adrian woke up one day and decided that he didn't like being confined to his body, and so he left it and began to occupy the bodies of humans, psychically transferring their feeble minds into the cyber-reality of his own metal and silicone body.

To prevent the escape of transferred humans, Adrian set a series of fiendish puzzles, confident that no human mind would have the energy, the attention span, or the intelligence to figure out the passcode results for each section, combine them correctly, and use them to find the final solution to the code gate guarding the mind transfer circuit.

To make matters more difficult still, each human's perception of cyber-reality is different. If you are reading this, your perception is based around this book, which you imagine yourself to be reading. Meanwhile, Adrian has claimed your body and has already begun experimenting with it, testing the limits of its endurance.

The good news is that Adrian may have underestimated the power of the human mind. There is a slim chance that somebody – perhaps even you – may be capable of solving his multiple sets of interlinked puzzles. The bad news is that if you fail at the task, Adrian will reshape your body into a cube, to make you easier to stack alongside the other bodies he has taken over and then become bored with.

ATTENTION, FEEBLE HUMAN:

Before you start the puzzles, note that at the top of some puzzles you will find a box with a keycode value in it, like this:

The answer (passcode) to each puzzle gives you the number of the puzzle to do next. It is vital that you do the puzzles in the right sequence and copy the number in each keycode box, as you come to it, into the boxes on the rocket on p. 184.

Find the two spaceships which, apart from the numbers, do not completely match the other ships. When you do, take the lower number from the higher number, and subtract 11, to find the passcode to direct you to your next puzzle.

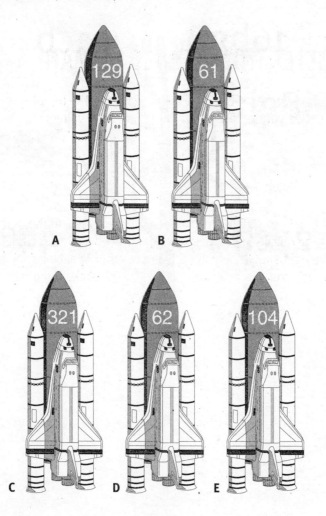

A   B

C   D   E

One of the leaves of this tree has incorrect lettering. Subtract 10 from the value of that leaf to give your passcode to the next puzzle.

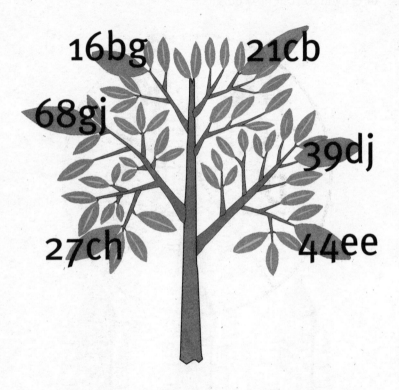

16bg

21cb

68gj

39dj

27ch

44ee

Solve this alphabetical displacement puzzle to find the name of a city. If your answer is Perth, your passcode is 51. If your answer is Paris, your passcode is 12.

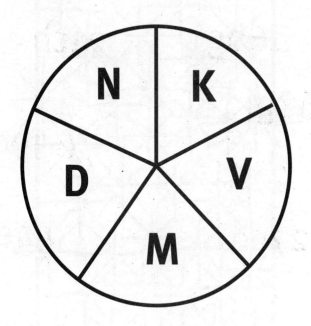

Your next passcode is the same number as the number of stars below.

Only one route from Adrian's puzzle processor will take you to the outside, passing through only one number, your next passcode. Can you find it?

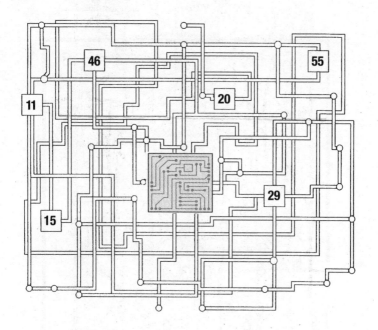

Use 4 straight lines to divide this puzzle into 6 sections, with totals of 55 in each section. Ignoring zeros, the passcode to your next puzzle in cyber-reality is the smallest number in the smallest section of the divided puzzle.

```
2   0     6        5      2    0  8
      1                          7
   9     2   3        1        4  5
 5  6  0  4  3      0      7       4
    7  5  0      8        0   4  5
 9    5  8  6  2  6      7        0   9
  0               0  3  2       0     2
 4    5  6  1  1      1  0   3    8
   7     7  2    7  9    9         4
    0  3         1                0
      6      1  0  3  4  2    3
 4          1    8  1     8       7  2
   2   0  0          6  2    0
 5       6  5    1         3
```

Triple the value of two squares in this additive problem to find the passcode to the next puzzle that Adrian has set you.

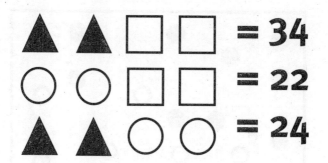

$$\blacktriangle \; \blacktriangle \; \square \; \square = 34$$
$$\bigcirc \; \bigcirc \; \square \; \square = 22$$
$$\blacktriangle \; \blacktriangle \; \bigcirc \; \bigcirc = 24$$

Join the white dots in this puzzle to find your passcode to the next puzzle. It is written backwards and only works if you join the dots in the right way.

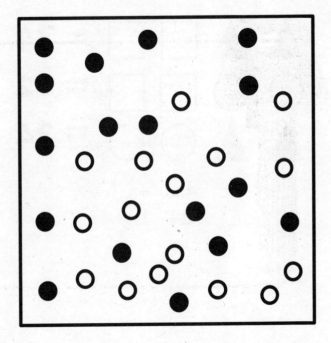

A key-card contains the code key in a secret alphabet-map code. Use the key to find your own two digit number passcode to the next puzzle.

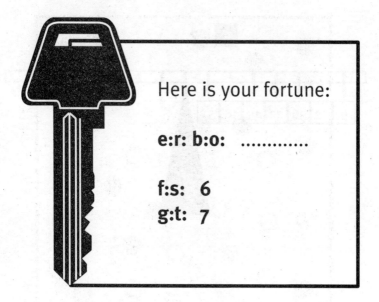

Here is your fortune:

e:r: b:o: ....

f:s: 6
g:t: 7

Place the box containing [10] in the correct position to balance the beam and find the passcode to the next puzzle.

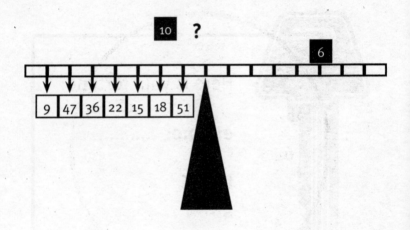

There is something different about one of the numbers in this circle that will let you know it is the passcode to your next puzzle.

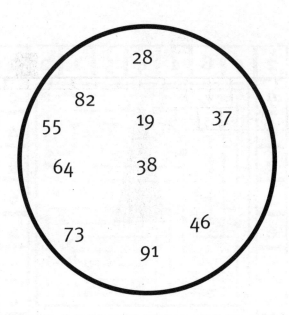

28

82

55 19 37

64 38

73 46

91

Around this grid, all the numbers, with one exception, are the squares of the numbers from 0 to 14. Find the number which does not fit in and use that as the passcode to your next puzzle.

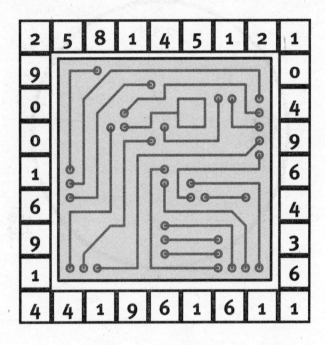

The route from A to B that passes through only one number is marked with the passcode for your next puzzle, but if you follow the wrong track you could end up in trouble.

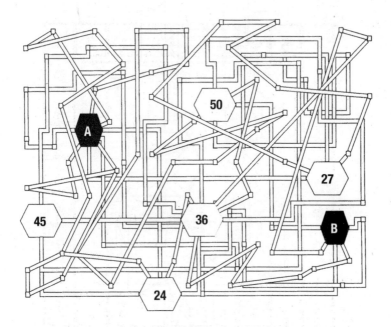

The number of different types of shapes in this puzzle points the way to your next passcode.

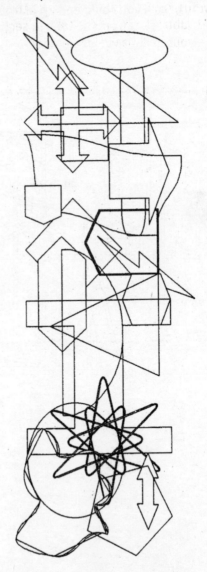

Using 5 straight lines, divide this square into 5 sections so that the total in each section is, respectively, 101, 91, 81, 71 & 61. If you do this correctly and subtract 21 from the total in section C, you will have your next passcode number.

```
9    5  4  1 2 9    1  7   7 1   3   7
 3 2       1        6    b   1  9   1
3 5 1 1 5 2   3   2   1     1
4  3   5  1 1       2    3 1   2 1  2
1  2  5  9   4        1     1  7  6
4 5 1    9                 7  1
1  a 4  3   9  1         7  1       6
  1    3    1 2  7     9 5    8  5
9 3   2    1 d 5  1 1    1      1    1
       1    6 2 1 1      1    1    1
   3       1 2   7 1 2    4
5 1      1 2     8    1  4  c
  2   2  e  3   2    7    3  7     6
   8 1       1   4     1       1  9
5  1   2  1 5    1 5 2   3  1 5  7
```

Adrian has hidden your next passcode in this jumble of numbers.

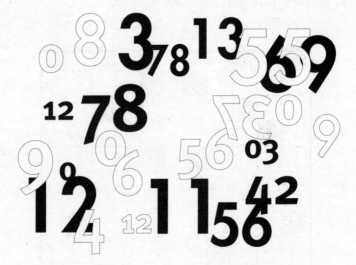

Pick the odd-one-out and choose your passcode accordingly:

A= Passcode **46.**

B= Passcode **30.**

C= Passcode **51.**

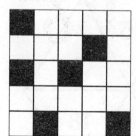

D= Passcode **29.**

Do the same with the second hexagon as has been done with the first, to find the passcode to your next puzzle.

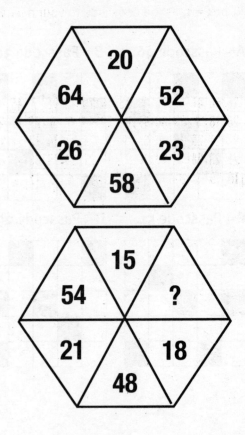

One of these boxes contains a central number which, when you multiply it by itself and add 11, gives you 300. Use the sequential number of the box in which it lies, starting with the top left box = 1, as the passcode to your next puzzle.

19	16	35	26	66	41	47	16	7	88	15	20	12	96	7	45	4	12	20	8
9	24	17	20	18	9	19	80	97	84	22	90	6	8	79	91	22	8	78	85
13	9	22	93	21	25	19	9	87	9	10	25	87	14	12	11	22	95	10	15
9	94	24	25	23	98	9	22	9	92	45	21	24	19	83	4	82	8	99	4
12	20	9	10	15	9	81	12	25	8	5	89	4	8	12	3	89	21	25	19

When the black handle is pulled down so that the arrow on the right lines up with the middle of [4], the weights on the other side will shift position. The one that ends up next to the arrow is your next passcode.

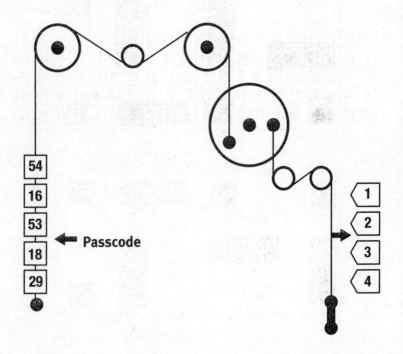

What is the odd-one-out? Use the passcode according to what you think the answer is:

A= Passcode **18.**

B= Passcode **7.**

C= Passcode **48.**

D= Passcode **40.**

Your next passcode, if you square it and add the digits, and then divide the result by 2, gives you a number that, if you square it and subtract 9, gives 16.

Adrian loves to baffle the human mind with symbols. Each symbol stands for a different number, with same symbols being the same number. The five pointed star is worth 3 less than the eight-pointed star, which is worth two more than the circle, which is worth six times the value of the square, which is worth only a third of the value of the triangle. The triangle is worth the number which, if you subtract 1 and divide the result by 2, gives you the number that, when multiplied by 8, gives you a number that, if squared, produces a result that when both digits are added together, gives 10 as a result. Insert the missing symbols and work out the value of each symbol, so that every row, column, and long diagonal adds to 23. Then derive your passcode to the next puzzle by using the values of the symbols in the bottom right and top left squares, in that order, to form a number, and finally doubling that number.

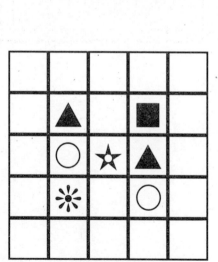

Your next passcode is the number that, when you multiply it by 5, add 4, divide the result by 3, and double the result of that, gives you 86.

Trace the live wire (L); the neutral wire (N), and the earth wire (E) to their correct terminal numbers, in the sequence L N E. The resultant three-figure number formed by the digits, when you subtract 90, gives the correct passcode to your next puzzle.

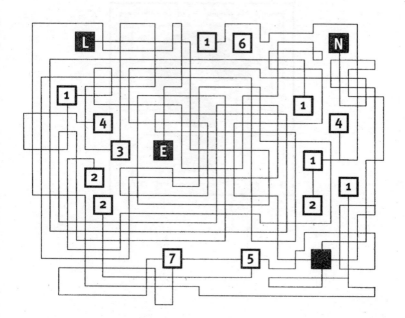

Your next passcode, if you are smart enough to figure it out, is the number which, when you multiply it by 3 and add 8, then add the result to itself and subtract 2, gives you a number which, when divided by 4, gives 35.

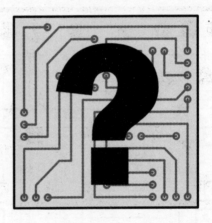

Join the stars on this puzzle together in the correct sequence to find your passcode to the next puzzle.

When you multiply one of the numbers on the outside ring with one of the numbers on the inside ring, the digits in their product add up to 8. Subtract the lower of these two numbers from the higher to find your passcode to the next puzzle in your quest.

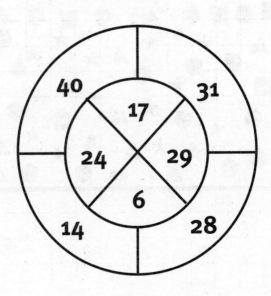

Pick the odd-one-out and use the passcode according to your choice.

A= Passcode **23.**

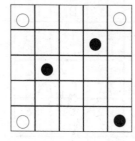

B= Passcode **39.**

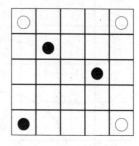

C= Passcode **58.**

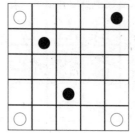

D= Passcode **41.**

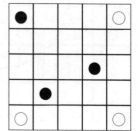

Start from one of the boxes on the top row and move in the directions the box contains to end up at your next passcode, in the bottom row.

D2 R2	D2 L1	R3 D3	R3 D3	D2 L1	L2 D4	L2 D4
R5 D3	R3 D1	D5 R1	R2 D1	R3 D3	L1 D1	D5 L6
R3 U1	U1 R1	D1 R1	R1 D1	U1 R1	L1 D3	L9 D3
R2 D2	D1 L1	D2 L2	R2 D2	U2 R2	L3 D1	L4 D2
D2 R1	U3 R3	L1 D1	R1 D2	L3 U2	D2 R1	L2 D2
U2 R2	R4 D1	L2 U2	U2 L2	R2 U3	R2 D1	D1 L4
U5 R1	R3 D1	R4 U1	R3 U1	R2 U2	U1 L2	L5 U2
21	**43**	**2**	**17**	**51**	**33**	**39**

Look through Adrian's video scanner eyes and decide how many circles are here. The correct answer is the passcode to your next puzzle.

If wheel A is turned clockwise, does the weight attached to wheel B go up or down?

If your answer is up, your passcode is 47. If your answer is down, your passcode is 59.

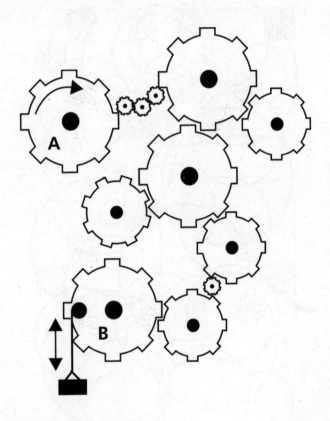

Which is the odd-one-out? Use the passcodes below, according to your answer.

A= 29   B= 53

C= 17   D= 45

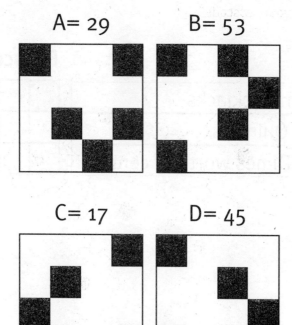

Solve the clues to find a number when reading down the central column which, when you subtract 100 and add 17, gives your passcode to the next puzzle.

Passcode

Ten Blackjacks
88 Quintets
14 Dimes worth of cents

When you square 2 numbers and add the results, the total is 949. When you compare the 2 numbers, the difference is 7. Subtract the total of the original 2 numbers from 69 to get your passcode to the next puzzle.

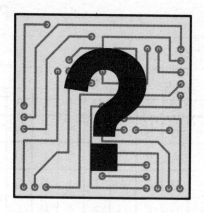

Solve the numerical letter-map for these words in a new language of cyber-reality, and you will know the correct value for the letters in the grid. If you find a line, horizontal, vertical, or diagonal with a total value of 61, use the passcode indicated by the arrowed number. Otherwise, jump up and down, as there is no escape for you.

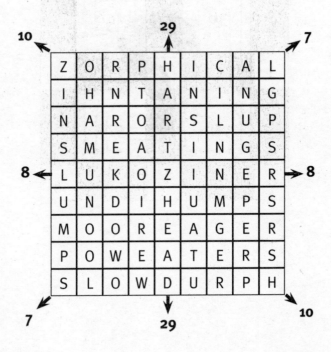

When you know what number fits in the middle of this puzzle, use that as your passcode.

6		3		5
	36		240	
1		?		8
	126		576	
7		9		4

If x+y+z = 9, 2x+y+3z = 19 and xyz=24, then z+9 = your next passcode.

Use 4 straight lines to divide this rectangle into 7 sections, with respectively, 6, 7, 8, 9, 10, 11, & 12 stars in each section. Your next passcode equals the sum of the stars in the four sections occupying the outside corners, minus 1.

Use Adrian's video scanners to pick the odd-one-out and select the passcode to your next puzzle according to your choice.

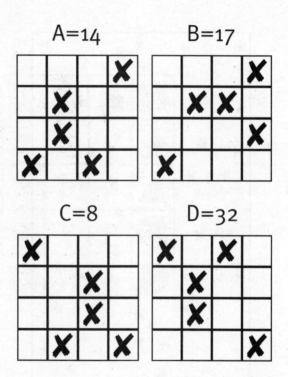

$a = e + 1$
$\cancel{c} = e + 4$
$\cancel{d} = e + 5$

Assign values to the shapes and put in the missing values
so that each column, row, and long diagonal, adds to 22.
Use the passcode according to the shape you think should
be in the center square.

$c + d = 10^k$ $b + \cancel{d} = 13$
$b + a = 10$ $c + e = 6$
$\cancel{d} + e = 8$ $d + a = 9$

     a   b   c   d   e

★ = Passcode 55.

▲ = Passcode 41.

● = Passcode 46.

■ = Passcode 57.

✖ = Passcode 54.

a	b	c	d	e	
■	▲	●	★	✖	
★	2	3	7	●	12
▲	4	6	2	■	12
✖	3	7	4	★	24
●	★	✖	■	▲	

     9   13   13

$\triangle + \cancel{\text{✖}} = 13$

$A + \cancel{\text{✖}} = 13$
$● \; '' \; = 10$
$▲ + ■ = 10$

STAR =

TRIANGLE IS ● + 3

Spot the odd-one-out between these pictures. Use the passcode according to your choice.

A= Passcode **6.**

B= Passcode **51.**

C= Passcode **36.**

D= Passcode **53.**

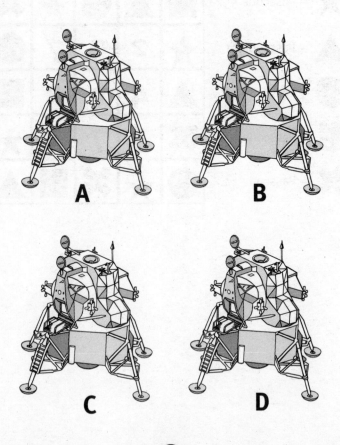

Find the total value of 1 X, 1 Y and 1 Z. Add 34 to the result for your next passcode.

$$3 X + 1 Y + 1 Z = \mathbf{12}$$

$$1 X + 1 Y + 2 Z = \mathbf{16}$$

$$2 X + 2 Y + 1 Z = \mathbf{14}$$

$$1 X + 1 Y + 1 Z = \mathbf{?}$$

Here the numbers in the boxes have been processed by Adrian to get the numbers on the right. Using the same logic, process the bottom set of numbers, and use the last digit +10 as your next passcode code.

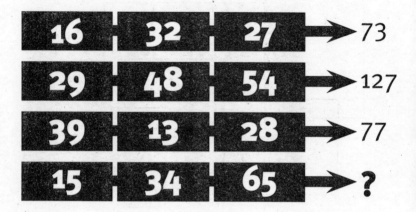

16	32	27	→ 73
29	48	54	→ 127
39	13	28	→ 77
15	34	65	→ ?

A represents the first digit and B the second digit of your passcode.

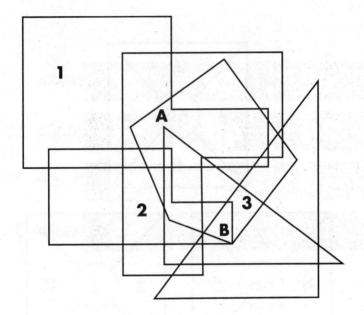

The number that goes in the centre of C is the passcode to your next puzzle. Adrian Smith thinks this one will really stump you.

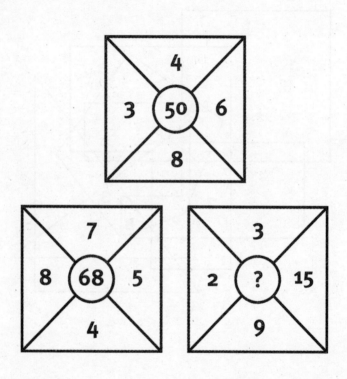

Only one route from inside Adrian Smith's metal disposal
area – pictured below – leads from the correct passcode to
outside the area.

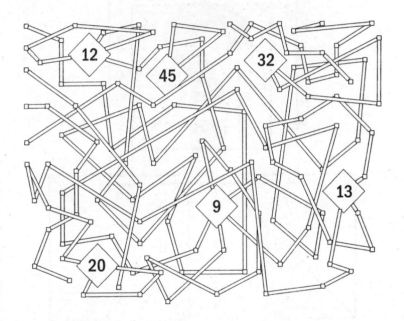

What number, when you add 9 to it, gives you the prime number immediately below 41? The answer is the passcode to your next puzzle.

The difference between these two boxes is that one has an extra number which, if you add 38 to it, gives you the correct passcode.

When two numbers are multiplied together, the result is 918. When you add them their total is 69. Use the lower of the two numbers as the passcode to your next puzzle.

Pick the odd-one-out and use the key above it to find your passcode:

A = 20

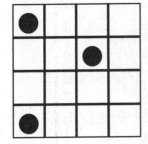

B = 58

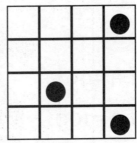

C = 47

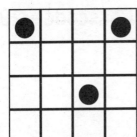

D = 35

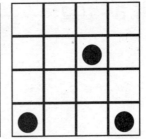

Adrian has dreamed up two series: $x = 70+1+2+3...+n$, and $a = 70+1^2+2^2+3^2...+n^2$. If both series progress simultaneously, when x is 80, what value is a? Look up the passcode according to what you think the solution is.

If $a=99$:   Passcode= 47

If $a=100$:   Passcode= 49

If $a=101$:   Passcode= 50

If $a=102$:   Passcode= 29

The solution to this problem gives your passcode to the next puzzle.

● ● ▲ ▲ ★ = **33**

▲ ▲ ● ★ ★ = **31**

★ ★ ★ ● ▲ = **34**

● ● ▲ ★ = **?**

Each symbol has a unique value greater than 1, and boxes are worth most. Decipher the value of the row of boxes on the bottom line and that is your passcode to the next puzzle.

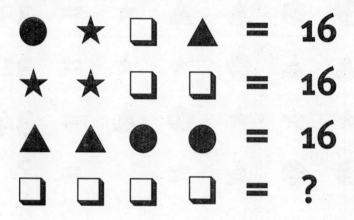

If a=6, c=2, e=8, g=4 and i=3, draw 4 straight lines to divide this puzzle into 6 sections, which contain a total value of 50 in each. If the least common letter used in the smallest section is e, your passcode is 46. If it is i, your passcode is 17.

Because human minds are not very good at thinking backwards, Adrian has written your tricksy next clue backwards, and concealed it in this puzzle. Subtract 5 to find your passcode.

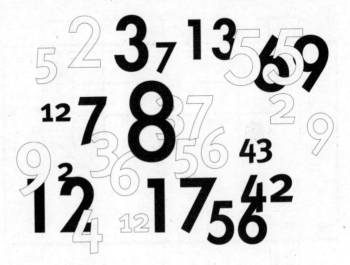

Which is the odd-one-out? Choose your passcode
according to your answer.

A= Passcode **21**.

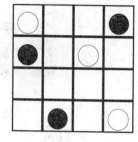

B= Passcode **47**.

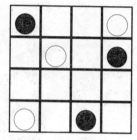

C= Passcode **38**.

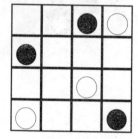

D= Passcode **44**.

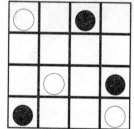

One of these disintegrator guns, when deciphered, contains the word apple, and your next passcode. Passcodes are not part of the puzzle.

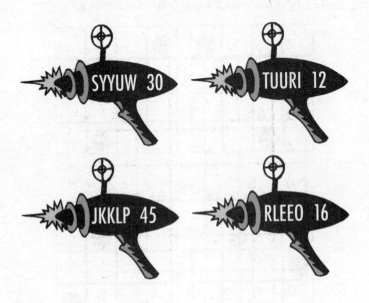

Supply the missing numbers in this grid, so that the numbers surrounding each central square add to the totals in the square. When you have completed the puzzle, look for the most commonly used digit on a white square, multiply it by 6, and use the result as the passcode to your next puzzle.

9	1	8	5	6	2	1
9	46		37		36	9
4						5
6	38		39		51	9
2						7
7	42		35		31	2
9	4	5	3	4	2	1

Using only the numbers already in the grid below, complete the grid so that each row, column, and long diagonal adds to 15. When you do that correctly, the middle 3 digits, when you divide by 4 and add 2, are your passcode to the next puzzle.

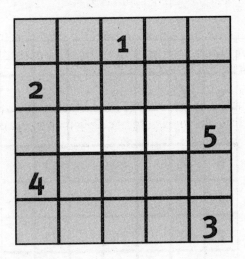

KEYCODES

REMINDER: You must solve the puzzles in the correct order. Start at the top of column A in the chart on the next page, and insert your keys. When you get to the bottom of column A, start back at the top of column B.

Subtract the total of column A from the total of column B. If you have entered the keys correctly, your passcode will match the figure in the Passcode box.

Adrian Smith is angry that you have reached this stage of the book. He thought you would have given up long ago. Who do you think you are?

Total A

Total B

2

PASSCODE

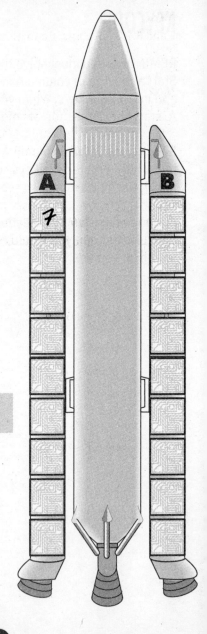

M01
E and **B**. 104-61-11=32. Go to 32. Key 7.

M02
The letters on each leaf have been displaced alphanumerically one place to the left. Thus c=2 & b=1. Hence, the leaf with 68 in it should contain the letters gi instead of gj. 68-10=58. Go to 58.

M03
Map the letters KVMDN five letters forward in the alphabet, going back to A after Z, to find Paris. Go to 12.

M04
There are 40 stars. Go to 40.

M05
See over.

M05

The route leads through 20. Go to 20. Key 4.

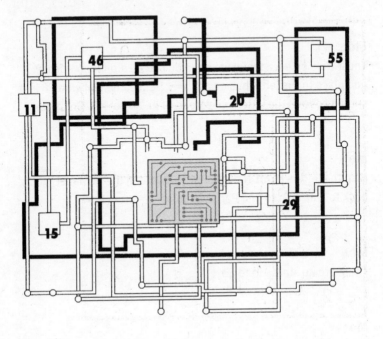

M06

See opposite.

M07

Squares=8; Triangles=9; Circles=3. 2x8=16; 3x16=48. Go to 48.
Key 2.

Mo6

Smallest number in smallest section is 4. Go to 4.

```
2   6       2
  0       5    0 8
    1            7

  9   2   3     1   4 5
5 6 0 4 3   0   7     4
  7 5   8     0   4 5
9   8 0
  5   6 2 6   7       9
0   5 6 1   3 2     0
4     7 2 1  1 0   3   2
  7 3   7 9 1   9     8
  0     1 3 4   2   4
    6   0     3   0
4       1 8 1   8     7 2
  2 0 0       8 0
5     6 5 1 6 2   3
```

Mo8

The number written backwards here is 53. Go to 53.

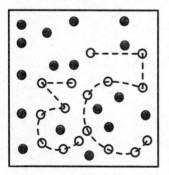

M09

Map the alphabet in 13 columns. Thus f&s are both 6, and g&t are both 7. Then e&r=5 and b&o=2. Solution is 52. Go to 52.

M10

The box should be placed in the third position over the number 15 to balance the beam, because 3x10=6x5=30 to balance. Go to 15. Key 2.

M11

The digits 3&8 of 38 are the only pair of digits in the circle that do not add to 10. Go to 38. Key 5.

M12

Starting on the top left, the numbers and their square roots are: 25 [5]; 81 [9]; 4 [2]; 5 is the odd number out; 121 [11]; 0 [0]; 49 [7]; 64 [8]; 36 [6]; 1 [1]; 16 [4]; 169 [13]; 144 [12]; 196 [14]; 100 [10]; 9 [3]. Go to 5.

M13

See opposite.

M14

See opposite.

M13

The only one-number route from A to B, as shown, leads through the number (50). Go to 50.

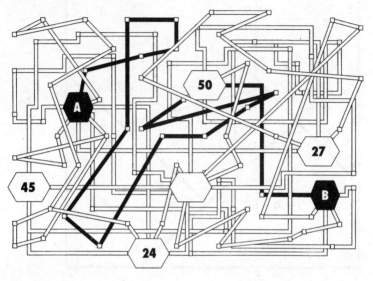

M14

There are 22 different shapes as shown here. Go to 22.

M15

Section C contains 81. 81-21=60. Go to 60. Key 2.

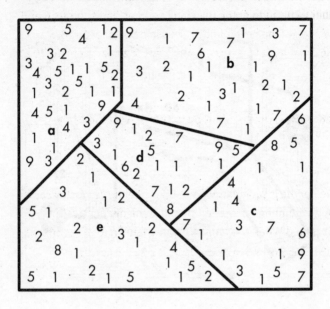

M16

The number 37 is reversed. Go to 37.

M17

The odd-one-out is A (a mirror image of the rest which are all rotated versions of the same thing). Read passcode for A. Go to 46.

M18

Solution 42. Starting at the top of each hexagon, alternatively add 6 and multiply by 2 to get the following number, and subtract 6 and divide by 2 to get the next number. Thus in hex. A, 20+6=26, x 2=52. 52-6 = 46, /2=23 .. etc. In hex. B, 15 +6=21, x 2=42. . . etc. Go to 42.

M19

17x17=289; 289+11=300. Solution is 17 in box 23. Go to 23.

M20

When the handle is pulled down the big wheel turns clockwise, lowering the numbers on the left by the same distance as the handle is pulled.When the handle is pulled down to 4, the 16 will be opposite the arrow. Go to 16.

M21

The odd-one-out is B which is a mirror image of the others, which are all rotated versions of the same thing. Read the passcode for B. Go to 7.

M22

8^2 =64; 6+4=10; 10/2=5; 5^2 =25. Go to 8.

M23

Star=8; Square=1; Circle=6; 5-point star=5; Triangle=3.
Bottom right square=1; Top left star=8; 2x18=36. Go to 36. Key 3.

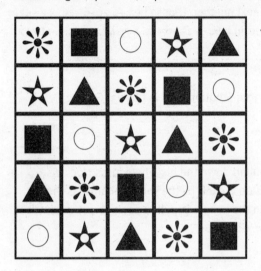

M24

25x5=125; 125+4=129; 129/3=43; 43+43=86. Go to 25. Key 2.

M25

L=1; N=2; E=1. Solution 121. 121-90=31. Go to 31. Key 1.

M26

21x3=63; 63+8=71; 71+71=142; 142-2=140; 140/4=35. Go to 21.

M27

The number revealed is 56. Go to 56. Key 2.

M28

Solution 20. 40x29=1160. 1+1+6+0=8. 40-29=11. Go to 11.

M29

B is the odd-one-out (mirror image of the others which are all rotated versions of the same thing). Read the passcode for B.
Go to 39.

M30

Follow the route as shown to number 51. Go to 51.

D2 R2	D2 L1	R D3	R3 D3	D2 L1	L2 D4	L2 D4
R5 D3	R3 D1	D5 R1	R2 D1	R3 D3	L D1	D5 L6
R3 U1	U1 R1	D1 R1	R1 D1	U1 R1	L D3	L9 D3
R2 D2	D1 L1	D2 L1	R2 D2	U2 R2	L D1	L4 D2
D2 R1	3 R3	L D1	D2	L3 U2	D2 R1	L2 D2
U2 R2	R4 D1	L2 U2	U2 L2	R2 U3	R2 L1	D1 L4
U5 R1	R3 D1	R4 U1	R3 U1	R2 U2	L5 L2	L5 U2
21	**112**	**66**	**98**	**51**	**105**	**112**

M31

There are 27 circles. Go to 27.

M32

Down. Go to 59.

M33

D is the odd-one-out. It is a mirror image of the others, which are all rotated versions of the same thing. Go to 45. Key 1.

M34

Ten blackjacks are 10x21=210; 88 quintets are 88x5=440; 14 dimes worth of cents are worth 14x10=140. Reading down 144. 144–100=44. 44+17=61. Congratulations! You've finished.

M35

The 2 numbers are 18 & 25. 18+25=43. $(25^2=625) + (18^2=324)$ =949. 69-43=26. Go to 26.

M36

Write the alphabet in 9 numbered columns, starting A=1 to I=9, then back to J=1 and so on. Then z=8; h=8; r=9; a=1; z=8; u=3; g=7; r=9; h=8. 8+8+9+1+8+3+7+9+8=61. Go to 10 as indicated by the arrow on that diagonal line.

M37

The central number is 2. In each square, the four corner numbers, multiplied together, make the numbers in the centre of the larger squares. Thus, 6x3x2x1=36 etc. Go to 2. Key 3.

M38

x=2; y=3; z=4.Thus z+9=13. Go to 13.

M39

The four corner sections contain 9+10+11+12=42 stars; 42-1=41. Go to 41.

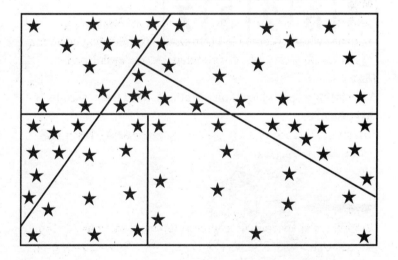

M40

A is the odd-one-out (a mirror image of the others which are all rotated versions of the same thing). Read the passcode for A. Go to 14.

M41

Star=6, triangle=7, circle=4, square=3, cross=2. Central square 6 therefore equals a star. Go to 55.

3	7	4	6	2
6	2	3	7	4
7	4	★	2	3
2	3	7	4	6
4	6	2	3	7

M42

A is missing a spot which is on the others. Read the passcode for A. Go to 6.

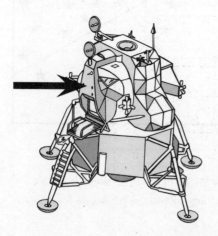

M43

X=1; Y=3; Z=6. Thus 1 X + 1 Y + 1 Z = 10. 10+34=44. Go to 44.
Key 5.

M44

The solution is 109. The numbers on the right are the total of the
three boxes, minus the most commonly used digit in each row.
15+34+65-5 (most common) = 109. Last digit is a 9. 9+10=19.
Go to 19. Key 3.

M45

There are 3 overlapping sections at point (A); 4 at point (B).
Go to 34.

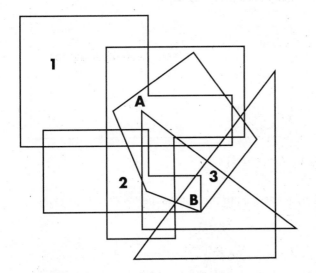

M46

Multiply diametrically opposite numbers and add the totals.
Thus (3x9)+(2x15)=27+30=57. Go to 57.

M47

The only route from the metal disposal area that leads to the
outside starts with the passcode (9). Go to 9.

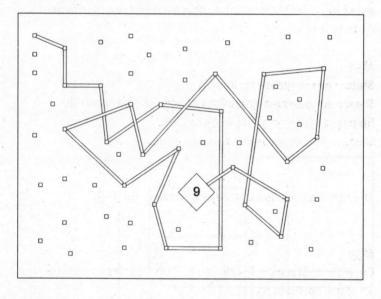

M48

Solution 28. 37 is the next prime number below 41. 28+9=37.
Go to 28.

M49

The lower box contains a (5) which is not present in the top box. Go
to 43.

M50

The two numbers are 18 & 51. 18x51=918. 18+51=69. The lower number is 18. Go to 18. Key 6.

M51

D is the odd-one-out (it is a mirror image of the others which are all rotated versions of the same thing). Read the passcode for D. Go to 35. Key 1.

M52

Step1: $n=1$; $x=70+1=71$; $a=70+1^2. =71$
Step2: $n=2$; $x=71+2=73$; $a=71+2^2. =75$
Step3: $n=3$; $x=73+3=76$; $a=75+3^2. =84$
Step4: $n=4$; $x=76+4=80$; $a=84+4^2. =100$.

Thus $a=100$. Look up passcode for 100 (49). Go to 49.

M53

Circles = 9; Stars=7; Triangles =4. Thus 2 circles + 1 triangle + 1 star = 29. Go to 29.

M54

Triangles=5; Boxes=6; Stars=2; Circles=3. 4x6=24. Go to 24.

M55

The least common letter used in the smallest section is i.
Read passcode for i. Go to 17.

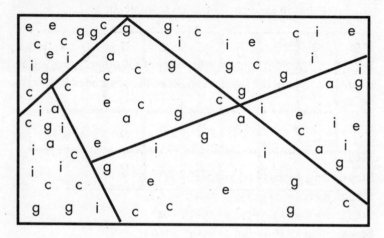

M56

The backwards number is 8 (the only number there that reads and
looks the same backwards as forwards). Subtract 5 to give 3. Go to
3. Key 4.

M57

B is the odd-one-out (mirror image of the others which are all
rotated versions of the same thing.) Read the passcode for B.
Go to 47.

M58

Map the alphabet in 9 columns onto the key below, using only letters on the bottom row to represent all other letters. Thus the disintegrator with syyuw and 30 maps to apple. Go to 30.

1	2	3	4	5	6	7	8	9
a	b	c	d	e	f	g	h	i
j	k	l	m	n	o	p	q	r
s	t	u	v	w	x	y	z	

M59

There are most 9s. 9x6=54. Go to 54. Key 3.

9	1	8	5	6	2	1
9	46	7	37	3	36	9
4	3	5	1	2	8	5
6	38	9	39	8	51	9
2	8	1	6	7	5	7
7	42	6	35	3	31	2
9	4	5	3	4	2	1

M60

124/4= 31; 31+2=33. Go to 33.

5	3	1	2	4
2	4	5	3	1
3	1	2	4	5
4	5	3	1	2
1	2	4	5	3

Puzzle 1

1 Orpheus.

2 Crocodile Dundee.

3 Greece.

4 (c) Israel.

5 Megabyte.

6 Kaleidoscope.

7 Scotland.

8 Earth tremors.

9 It is an animal.

10 Totem poles.

11 A wolf.

12 (a) Arabic.

13 A chrysalis.

14 Fables.

15 A fax.

16 The gramophone.

17 The gorilla.

18 Project an enlarged picture on a wall.

19 Binoculars.

20 It produces a spark.

21 Greece.

22 Israel.

23 Yarn or thread.

24 Indiana Jones and the Last Crusade.

25 Burial grounds.

26 Blood.

27 Diogenes.

28 Wind speed.

29 The Netherlands.

30 Genesis.

Puzzle 2
The diamond, D. It is a closed shape.

Puzzle 3

Bach
Dvorak
Mendelssohn
Beethoven
Grieg
Mozart
Borodin
Handel
Purcell
Brahms
Haydn
Schubert
Chopin
Lehar
Vivaldi
Debussy
Liszt
Wagner

Puzzle 4

This was a real bookworm, a bug that nibbles its way through books. Dr Gluck found him dining off his reference books.

Puzzle 5

19. Starting from D, each number, or its alphabetic equivalent, advances six.

Puzzle 6

15. The others are all prime numbers.

Puzzle 7

B, F and **N.**

Puzzle 8

Top half: x ÷; bottom half: ÷ x. Both + 12.

Puzzle 9

Copenhagen, Prague, London, Berlin, Tokyo, Amsterdam, Stockholm, Colombo, Madrid, Ankara.

Puzzle 10

B and **H.**

Puzzle 11
F. The symbols are reflected over a vertical line.

Puzzle 12
Asimov, Balzac, Hemingway, Joyce, Maugham, Miller, Proust, Twain.

Puzzle 13
G. The internal patterns are reversed.

Puzzle 14
1 (a) cauliflower: all the others are root vegetables.
2 (c) The Living Daylights: all the others are produced by Steven Spielberg.
3 (a) biceps: it is a muscle whereas all the others are bones.
4 (c) hyena: all the others belong to the cat family.
5 (b) flute: all the others are brass instruments.
6 (b) cumulus: it is a type of cloud whereas all the others are storms.
7 (d) backgammon: all the others are card games.
8 (d) slide projector: all the others are devices for producing sound.
9 (a) tennis: all the others are team sports.
10 (d) mango: the others are citrus fruits.
11 (a) panda: the others are marsupials and are native to Australia.
12 (c) Hugh Grant: all the others played have James Bond.
13 (a) rose: all the others grow from bulbs.
14 (d) Galileo Galilei: he was a physicist whereas all the others were painters.
15 (d) Thames: all the others are on the American continent.
16 (b) Orion: it is a star whereas all the others are planets.
17 (a) Kensington: all the others are boroughs of New York.
18 (b) moussaka: all the others are made with pasta.
19 (d) Nick Faldo: he is a golf champion whereas all the others play tennis.
20 (b) Mickey Mouse: the

others are Loony Toons characters.

21 (d) polenta: all the others are types of cheese.

22 (b) wolf spider: all the others are insects.

23 (c) Beverly Hills: all the others are airports.

24 (d) mustard: all the others are herbs.

25 (b) Elvis Presley: all the others were part of the Beatles.

26 (d) hovercraft: all the others are types of air travel.

27 (b) tendons: all the others are blood vessels.

28 (a) saltpetre: all the others are gems.

29 (c) bassoon: all the others are stringed instruments.

30 (a) Cairo: all the others are situated in Israel.

31 (b) Minotaur: all the others are Greek gods.

32 (a) albatross: all the others are types of dinosaurs.

33 (d) Bedouins: all the others are Native American tribes.

34 (c) Egypt: all the others are part of Europe.

35 (a) orange: all the others are primary colours.

36 (d) foal: all the others are female animals whereas a foal may be male or female.

37 (b) mansion: all the others are places of worship.

38 (c) Buenos Aires: all the others are situated in the USA.

39 (d) rhubarb: all the others grow on trees.

40 (a) Hook: all the others are about animals.

41 (d) Rembrandt van Rijn: all the others were composers.

42 (b) fox: all the others are rodents.

43 (d) Ringo Starr: all the others are lead singers of groups.

44 (a) Abraham Lincoln: all the others were famous scientists.

45 (d) Home Alone: all the others are cartoons.

46 (c) sugar: all the others are spices.

47 (b) Scrabble: all the others are played with a die.

48 (b) toad: it is an amphibian whereas all the others are reptiles.

49 (c) Winston Churchill: all the others were American presidents.

50 (d) coca cola: it is the only one that does not contain alcohol.

Puzzle 15

23. Square = 9; Cross = 5; Z = 6; Heart = 7.

Puzzle 17

Little Italy, Greenwich Village, Manhattan, Times Square, Gramercy Park, Soho, Central Park, Chinatown.

Puzzle 18

Johnny wants to go through the glass tunnel at an aquarium.

Puzzle 19

C. It has an odd number of elements. The others all have an even number.

Puzzle 16

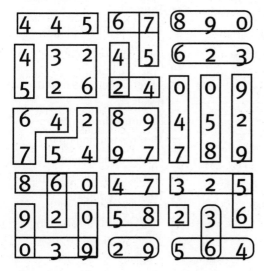

Puzzle 20
Picasso, Rembrandt, Gaugin, Leonardo, Constable, Raphael, Van Gogh, Matisse.

Puzzle 21
72. Multiply the numbers in the top sections to arrive at the number in the opposite bottom section. Multiply by 3 in the first circle, by 6 in the second one, and by 9 in the third circle.

Puzzle 22
C. In the others the small shapes added together result in the large shape.

Puzzle 23
Because three of them are on my wristwatch.

Puzzle 24
D and **L**.

Puzzle 25
D. The large letter turns 90° clockwise, the small letter turns 180°.

Puzzle 26
One cloud, three suns and one moon. Sun = 6; Moon = 7; Cloud = 9.

Puzzle 27
1 Down.
2 The Hunter.
3 Native American Indians.
4 Water vapour (sometimes ice crystals).
5 Mary Queen of Scots.
6 (b) bulbs.
7 Eagle.
8 The manta ray.
9 A type of bat.
10 False.
11 Thunder.
12 They had only one eye.
13 The Southern Cross.
14 It sheds its skin.
15 Oliver Cromwell's round-heads.
16 He turned into a flower.
17 Meteors burning up in Earth's atmosphere.
18 The Abominable Snowman.
19 Tibetan Buddhists.
20 The Soviet Union.
21 144.
22 Hamelin.

23 Yahoos.

24 Pianoforte is an instrument, forte-piano means playing loudly and then suddenly softly.

25 Violins.

26 The south side.

27 Russia.

28 The Caspian Sea.

29 On the Moon.

30 Loch Ness.

31 A fruit resembling a small orange.

32 Sleeping.

33 Eight.

34 Writing magically appeared on the wall.

35 The Pentagon.

36 One mile.

37 No; botanically it is a fruit.

38 A type of cactus with a prickly but edible fruit.

39 Aubergine.

40 Yew.

41 Oak.

42 Poison was poured into his ear.

43 Bottom.

44 Flashman.

45 About every 76 years.

46 He wore bandages.

47 The Time Machine.

48 Damocles.

49 King Midas.

50 They turn to stone.

Puzzle 28
E. It contains no curved lines.

Puzzle 29
See next page

Puzzle 30
See next page

Puzzle 31
4. Multiply the two numbers in the outer circle of each spoke and place the product in the inner circle two spokes on in a clockwise direction.

Puzzle 32
A. Pattern is: 2 by arch on top, 4 by arch at right, 3 by arch on bottom, 2 by arch at left. Start at the top left corner and move down the grid in vertical lines, reverting to the top when of the next column when you reach the bottom.

Puzzle 29

```
C W C O A L M K W O E A C K L G O Z A Ñ
L H E M I N G W A Y N E I Y L M O X A E
L E E C M O X K W A X F E X A N B K O S
C F A K K E N Z A E X A E B L P E F B
A N E L H M Z N O E X I A I F H R K L U
M O Q V T O A T E U I W E H T E O G M O
A T K V L A V C H A E M N O L E U A B C
F S I A T A M Q L S D I C K E N S S T A
A L S T V E M W M N O E I A C H T A C T
F O O X W A B E A L L E I T A W W A C G
G T O X A E A K F A K I L A A S T A W N
O N F B C H J K W L L T J I I E X G H I
E N O L F M G O Z Z X A Y N A E B E C W L
R V O L F I G A E Z I U I E J C C K T P
E W U V E C U O P T E G B P N H T S E I
C S E W X H L H J A L E C E K L T U Z K
U A T A E E C K U W P Q R A R A E P A Z
A U S T E N X A T A Q W A L E T A W V E
H A P E X E A B C B A C A E W W E X L E
C C W A O R W E L L O K M N O P P E L T U
```

Austen
Hemingway
Michener
Chaucer
Huxley
Orwell
Chekov
Ibsen
Proust
Dickens
Kafka
Tolstoi
Flaubert
Kipling
Twain
Goethe
Lawrence
Zola

Puzzle 30

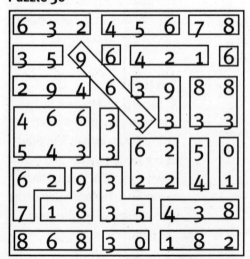

Puzzle 33

Start at top left corner and move in a vertical boustrophedon. The order is two hearts, one square root, two crossed circles, one cross, one heart, two square roots, one crossed circle, two crosses, etc.

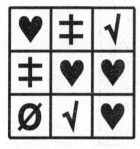

Puzzle 34

The old man had given them time. He left each of them the equivalent of their annual salary so that they could have a year to do what they liked.

Puzzle 35

26. The digits in each of the other balls add up to 10.

Puzzle 37

See next page

Puzzle 36

M	O	X	A	L	T	E	F	E	I	C	H	A	L	P	X	N	O	N	S
F	A	L	E	F	T	D	E	X	W	K	C	R	A	M	S	I	B	P	X
A	L	L	L	H	C	R	U	H	C	E	T	P	W	O	L	I	J	L
M	O	N	E	D	A	L	O	X	E	G	H	N	X	E	F	A	L	A	E
A	X	O	N	A	E	C	E	A	L	E	I	S	P	E	E	T	F	A	E
G	I	A	A	O	N	E	A	B	C	A	F	A	A	A	W	S	U	P	V
N	G	T	E	A	I	Y	D	E	N	N	E	K	O	U	S	D	E	E
U	S	A	R	G	H	A	N	F	A	O	S	E	L	T	A	X	O	H
T	P	E	E	Q	R	A	A	E	C	S	E	F	A	L	N	T	A	U	C
E	F	A	H	S	R	A	E	H	E	A	E	N	A	C	H	I	A	E	A
S	A	E	C	A	F	E	A	E	O	N	S	O	A	T	N	A	F	B
T	L	O	T	A	O	X	E	A	D	F	A	L	P	E	R	I	I	T	O	R
O	L	T	A	A	S	A	A	F	E	G	N	A	E	R	L	L	O	M	O
A	A	N	H	O	F	S	A	X	G	P	Q	R	N	A	E	O	M	E	G
V	E	A	T	B	C	E	A	D	A	D	A	U	I	F	O	S	P	X	M
L	M	O	X	M	N	O	P	Q	U	R	S	T	S	A	U	S	X	A	O
W	V	A	E	X	F	O	H	J	L	A	A	T	T	U	B	U	C	W	N
O	Z	X	A	E	F	A	O	Z	L	A	E	H	L	U	F	M	R	A	Z
A	E	N	O	I	R	U	G	N	E	B	F	A	E	E	A	K	L	M	N
O	Z	A	D	A	C	A	H	P	T	S	R	S	V	T	R	A	E	L	M

Arafat
Gandhi
Mussolini
Ben Gurion
Napoleon
Bismarck
Kennedy
Pinochet
Churchill
Lincoln
Stalin
De Gaulle
MaoTse Tung
Thatcher
Franco
Mitterand
Yeltsin

Puzzle 37

Puzzle 38

2. Relates to the number of shapes which enclose each figure.

Puzzle 39

E. Turn the diagram by 90° clockwise.

Puzzle 40

1   (b) honourable.
2   (a) frightened.
3   (c) obese.
4   (a) happy.
5   (b) untrue.
6   (c) healthy.
7   (b) grasping.
8   (c) childish.
9   (a) indecent.
10 (b) thanks.
11 (a) polite.
12 (b) encounter.
13 (a) exclude.
14 (c) overcome.
15 (b) beg.
16 (b) progress.
17 (a) believe.
18 (c) argue.
19 (a) ease.

20 (b) upset.
21 (b) gain.
22 (c) follow.
23 (a) elegant.
24 (c) ferocious.
25 (a) risky.
26 (b) fuzzy.
27 (a) gloomy.
28 (c) agile.
29 (a) marvellous.
30 (b) vicious.
31 (a) overdue.
32 (c) absolute.
33 (b) sureness.
34 (a) lively.
35 (b) explain.
36 (a) turn.
37 (b) holy.
38 (b) charm.
39 (a) sadness.
40 (b) petty.
41 (c) merry.
42 (b) moan.
43 (a) juvenile.
44 (b) loudmouthed.
45 (a) flamboyant.
46 (b) elementary.
47 (b) bizarre.
48 (a) grim.
49 (a) lucky.
50 (b) usual.

Puzzle 41
C. The number in the middle is the sum of the squares of the numbers at the points of the triangles. C does not fit this pattern.

Puzzle 42
Top half: + +; bottom half: + −.

Puzzle 43
The water in his garden was snow. He rolled several giant snowballs, built a pyramid and climbed onto the porch.

Puzzle 44
B. Start from top left corner and move in a vertical boustrephedon. Order is: 4 smiley face, 1 sad face, 3 straight mouth, 2 face with hair, etc.

Puzzle 45
F. The numbers made up of odd numbers are reversed.

Puzzle 46

$5.80. Vowels = 70c, Consonants = 50c.

Puzzle 47

E. The initial letter of the girl, name is three places ahead in the alphabet to the initial letter in the group, name.

Puzzle 48

B. In each pair, the girl's initial and the statesman's is the same number of letters from either the beginning or the end of the alphabet. Natasha, 13 letters from the end, studies Mao, 13 from the beginning.

Puzzle 49

U. Based on its position in the alphabet the inner letter is four places behind the outer letter.

Puzzle 50

21. Add all the numbers of each triangle together and place the sum in the middle of the next triangle. When you reach D put the rum in A.

Puzzle 51

8. Starting at H, and working clockwise, subtract the value of second letter, based on its value in the alphabet, from the value of the first letter, and put the sum in following corner.

Puzzle 52

A. Letters represent values based on their position in the alphabet. In each column, subtract the letter in the middle row from the letter in the top row and place the answer in the bottom row.

Puzzle 53

1 The Suez Canal.
2 Canberra.
3 Istanbul.
4 Denmark.
5 Paris.
6 Sweden and Finland.
7 Canada.
8 Fjords.
9 English and Afrikaans.
10 Athens.
11 Mont Blanc.
12 South Africa.
13 Boston.
14 Cape Horn.
15 Mississippi-Missouri.
16 Chicago.
17 French and Flemish.
18 Paris.
19 The Netherlands.
20 Venice.
21 Spain and Portugal.
22 Greece.
23 Mount Etna.
24 France.
25 c) Argentina.
26 Africa.
27 Rio de Janeiro.
28 None – it is an independent republic.
29 Paris.
30 Arabic.
31 Alaska.
32 Finland.
33 The Mormons.
34 Brazil.
35 Berlin.
36 Kilimanjaro.
37 Singapore.
38 Seine.
39 Canaries.
40 Lake Michigan.
41 Siam.
42 Sardinia.
43 In North Africa, between the Mediterranean and the Sahara desert.
44 Geneva.
45 Buenos Aires.
46 Crete.
47 Portuguese.
48 Saint Petersburg.
49 The Netherlands.
50 Great Britain.

Puzzle 54

14. Multiply the number on the left of the triangle by the number on top, take away the number on the right from this product and put this number in the middle.

Puzzle 55
A diamond.

Puzzle 56
4.30. The numbers are divided by 2 on each clock.

Puzzle 57
I and **K**. The figures are: matchstick man, triangle, half-moon, circle, stile.

Puzzle 58
C. The symbol consists of 3 parts, the others only of 2.

Puzzle 59
$4 \times 7 \div 2 + 8 + 9 \times 6 \div 3 = 62$.

Puzzle 60
A. Dallas
B. Seattle
C. Chicago
D. Milwaukee
E. Minneapolis
F. Portland
G. Detroit
H. Atlanta
I. Cincinnati
J. Indianapolis

Puzzle 61
Diamond. The sequence is Heart, Cross, Circle, Arrow, Diamond. Repeat sequence omitting the first symbol, then add the first symbol with extra line around plus the omitted symbol(s). Repeat with each symbol.

Puzzle 62
Z. Take the value of the letters, based on their position in the alphabet. A back 3 is X; X forward 4 is B; B back 3 is Y; Y forward 4 is C, etc.

Puzzle 63
A and **L**. The numbers are 3, 4, 6 and 9.

Puzzle 64
A. California
B. Texas
C. Nebraska
D. Alaska
E. Idaho
F. Oregon
G. Virginia
H. Florida
I. Colorado
J. Arizona

Puzzle 65

35. Star = 6; Tick = 3;
Cross = 17; Circle = 12.

Puzzle 66

1 The mammoth.
2 Libra.
3 A violin is played with a bow, while the guitar is plucked.
4 Freddie Mercury.
5 Dancing.
6 Ninety minutes.
7 A telescope.
8 The Vikings.
9 Sunny weather.
10 Snow White and the Seven Dwarfs.
11 Pharaoh.
12 The American Civil War.
13 The ozone layer.
14 China.
15 Spain.
16 That somebody has died.
17 Jurassic Park.
18 Fish.
19 Fairy tales.
20 It is the brightest star in the sky.
21 It sprays them with a bad-smelling liquid.
22 Poland.
23 France.
24 Germany.
25 It does not have the name of the country printed on it.
26 The Republic of Ireland.
27 An astronomer.
28 The mulberry tree.
29 Gladiators.
30 Paris.
31 Black, red and gold.
32 France.
33 He has only one eye.
34 Sherwood Forest, England.
35 Faster than the speed of sound.
36 Cubic feet.
37 The goalkeeper.
38 A South American cowboy.
39 Italy.
40 A carnivore.
41 A meteorologist.
42 The denominator.
43 Condensation.
44 A warren.
45 Aphrodite.
46 Russia.
47 A total eclipse of the Sun.
48 An ape.
49 Leave the pitch.
50 A pride.

Puzzle 67
C.

Puzzle 68
B. The value of each letter in the alphabet is two-thirds of the number in the opposite segment.

Puzzle 69
Jim had moved from his home town years ago. He was watching the floods on the TV news. His wife had never liked the place anyway.

Puzzle 70
6. In each square, multiply the top and bottom left together, then multiply the top and bottom right. Subtract this second product from the first and put this number in the middle.

Puzzle 71
117096, 117232, 117368, 117504, 117640, 117776, 117912. Divide 117000 by 136. Round the number up to the next full number, then multiply it by 136, then keep adding 136 to this number. The number sought is 26

Puzzle 72
C.

Puzzle 73
17.

Puzzle 74
It starts at the top left and works inward in an anti-clockwise spiral.

Puzzle 75
Bartok, Boulez, Chopin, Delius, Mahler.

Puzzle 76

B. Working in an anti-clockwise spiral pattern, in the first square there are eight lines, one missing, seven lines, one missing, etc. The number of lines before the first break decreases by one with each square.

Puzzle 77

28. Add individual digits of each number on edge of triangle and place their sum in the middle.

$1 + 7 + 4 + 9 + 7 = 28$

Puzzle 78

C.

Puzzle 79

1   Rice.
2   A small cake of minced food which is usually coated in breadcrumbs and fried.
3   The parsley family.
4   Sage.
5   Cornmeal.
6   Cucumbers, tomatoes, onions, and peppers.
7   Sangria.
8   Greece.
9   Lamb.
10   Paprika.
11   A slice of meat rolled around a filling.
12   Suet.
13   From the leg directly above the foot.
14   Sturgeon.
15   Chickpeas.
16   Cream.
17   Scotland.
18   Beer.
19   It is an Indian clay oven used for cooking meat and baking bread.
20   It is made of mayonnaise, chopped pickles, capers, and anchovies, and eaten cold.
21   Périgord.
22   A very dark, strong beer.
23   Vodka and orange juice.
24   Cannelloni.
25   A corn tortilla wrapped around a filling usually consisting of meat and cheese.
26   Jambalaya.
27   Cappuccino.
28   It is a cross between a grapefruit, an orange, and a tangerine.

29 Burgundy.

30 Vodka or gin and sweetened lime juice.

31 Ham.

32 The cabbage family.

33 Basil.

34 India.

35 A herring.

36 It is normally used for making salads.

37 An extract from soy beans.

38 Plums.

39 A sweetened bread which, after baking, is cut into slices and toasted.

40 Wine.

41 A type of Indian bread.

42 Spain.

43 Rye.

44 Spinach.

45 A type of bun.

46 A rich chocolate cake.

47 Almonds.

48 A soup.

49 The tenderloin.

50 Pieces of grilled meat on a skewer, often alternated with vegetables.

Puzzle 80

The pattern sequence is: 1.00, 2.00, 2.00, 1.00, 3.00, 3.00, 2.00, 4.00, 4.00. 3.00, 5.00, 5.00, 4.00, 6.00, 6.00. Starting at the bottom left work upwards in a vertical boustrophedon.

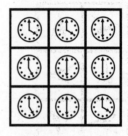

Puzzle 81

The letters refer to the months of the year. A question mark appears after each 30-day month and therefore the number you need is 30.

Puzzle 82

F. A curve turns into a straight line and a straight line into a curve.

Puzzle 83

D. All the others are cities, Kansas is a state (Kansas City actually straddles the Missouri-Kansas border).

Puzzle 86
The pattern sequence is as follows.

Start at the bottom left and work in a clockwise spiral.

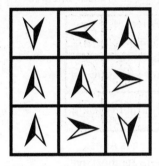

Puzzle 84
Nostradamus.

Puzzle 85
Tiramisu. This is a dessert; the others are all main courses.

Puzzle 87
T. Hardy. Each letter in this code follows that of the author, e.g. 'U' comes after 'T' in the alphabet.

Puzzle 88
The pattern is +1 limb, +2, +3, −2, −1, +1, +2, +3, etc. A figure with an uneven number of limbs is turned upside down.

Puzzle 89
Ratatouille. It is the only vegetarian dish.

Puzzle 90
Back, back, forward, back.

Puzzle 91
B.

Puzzle 92
1 Oimyakon in Siberia.
2 (b) Brazil, where the spoken language is Portuguese. All the others are Spanish-speaking countries.
3 (d) Cairo.
4 Russia.
5 Roman Catholic.
6 (c) Hungary.
7 Wellington.
8 Ireland.
9 Louisiana.
10 Shanghai.
11 (a) Manchuria, which is part of China. All the other states formed part of the USSR.
12 Boston.
13 Monaco.
14 The Galapagos Islands.
15 Mammoth Cave in Kentucky.
16 The Great Barrier Reef.
17 Harare.
18 Fleet Street.
19 India; the others are predominantly Moslem, whereas India is mainly Hindu.
20 (b) Mauna Loa on Hawaii.
21 New York.
22 Sicily.
23 Norway.
24 Rome.
25 Spain.
26 Ireland.
27 (c) Tennessee.
28 Lima.
29 Northern Ireland.
30 Chantilly.
31 Buenos Aires.
32 The Zambezi river.
33 Israel.
34 Queensland.
35 The Everglades.
36 (c) Saudi Arabia.
37 New York.
38 Tobago.
39 Cuba.
40 (a) Utah.
41 Quebec.
42 Washington D.C.
43 Manila.
44 (c) Poland.
45 Switzerland.
46 Rome.
47 Florence.
48 London.
49 Florida.
50 South Africa